MIRACLE
ON HAMMERTOWN ROAD

One Man's Fall and Salvation

MIRACLE
ON HAMMERTOWN ROAD

One Man's Fall and Salvation

JIM "BUBBA" BAY
WITH MIC RUZICH

ISBN: 978-1-58776-954-2

Library of Congress catalog card number: 2014941054

Manufactured in the United States of America
NetPublications, Inc.

675 Dutchess Turnpike, Poughkeepsie, NY 12603
www.hudsonhousepub.com
(800) 724-1100

Contents

This book is dedicated to my sons Robert and James Ulysses, and to my nephew Kahliff, and to all who have passed on too early.

And, as with everything in my life nowadays, I dedicate this book and any good that comes from it, to God.

Lord, My God, I cried out to You, and You healed me.
O Lord You lifted my soul up from the grave; You have kept me
alive, from among those gone down to the pit.

Psalm 30:2-3

Bubba, You Should Write a Book…

My nickname is Bubba. With a nickname like that, it's easy to guess that I've struggled with weight my entire life. When I graduated from high school I was pushing 300 pounds. During my first year in college, after a herculean regimen of so much running in place I burned though several pairs of sneakers, I lost more than 100 pounds. People told me I should write a book.

Sixteen years later, after my son James died in infancy, after I spent days and nights at the hospital at my little son's bedside, people told me I should write a book.

When my son Robert died six years after that due to complications from kidney disease at age 18, people told me I should write a book.

And when, after the night of November 15, 2009, when I came within a hairbreadth of death myself, almost everyone I told about that night said to me, 'Bubba, you *really* should write a book."

Me? Write a book? I doubted whether my life was worthy. But people were persistent. Bubba, you should write a book, they kept telling me. And so, finally, I have.

I CRIED OUT
TO YOU

THE FALL

November 15, 2009

I woke up, had breakfast, got washed up, then went about my day, never stopping for a moment to think that this day might be the most momentous of my life. But it would be. Forever after I would mark my life from this day forward.

I had recently separated from my wife, Yanina, who had brought our two children with her to Maine from upstate New York. Since I was feeling a little down, and with more free time than usual, I decided to get back to my favorite hobby- metal-detecting. I started metal-detecting when I was 22, and through the years I've had some great times and some great finds- buffalo nickels and Indian head pennies and colonial coppers. Odd though it seems to some, there's no greater thrill for me than to take something out of the ground that might have slipped out of George Washington's knickers. I also help people find things like septic systems, property markers, and lost keys and jewelry. I hadn't been metal-detecting much over the previous year, and so I decided to devote either a Saturday or Sunday each week to my hobby, and planned on packing a lunch and being out all day. I was also itching to go because I had recently found an internet forum on which I could post messages and pictures of my finds and chat with other metal-detecting enthusiasts. That day, November 15, 2009, was a typical November day in upstate New

York: sunny but brisk. It wasn't my best day in terms of finds, but being outdoors with the sun and wind on my face, the promise of finding buried and forgotten coins or rings or Revolutionary War musket shot, was enough to keep me out until twilight. I drove home with some Christian music on the radio, unloaded my equipment, and got washed up for dinner. More or less an ordinary day.

Since I'd been a bachelor again, dinner was usually one of my tuna specials or, to be perfectly honest, not-so-specials. And sure enough, after dinner I felt a little sick. So, in the hope of feeling better, I decided to go for a walk.

I'm a familiar sight in the neighborhood in my sweatpants and sneakers listening to music on my MP3 hoofing it along the town roads. I walk to control my weight, and also to clear my head. There have been times in my life when I'd walk almost every day after work. If it's dark, I usually drive to my parent's house, which is in town, and walk around under the street lights. I dress appropriately: sneakers, windbreaker, sweatpants. I walk against oncoming traffic, as you're supposed to do, or on the sidewalks in town. I usually walk for about an hour. But that night I was not doing my usual walk. I'd been out all day metal-detecting, so I'd had enough exercise; all I wanted was to get some air.

At around 7 o'clock I walked out toward the road that runs in front of my house, Route 199. It was dark, but I didn't bring a flashlight since the Pine Plains Town Hall is right across the street and they keep the lights on all night. A car was parked off the road, and a group of drunken men were stumbling around on the shoulder of Route 199. So I turned around and walked down Hammertown Road, back past my house. I walked down a small hill, then past my neighbor's house. I started to feel a bit better, so I turned around.

After I turned I saw in the distance the glare from approaching headlights. I crossed the road and started to walk, but the lights still seemed to be approaching. I thought it safer to step onto the shoulder of the road until the car passed. I took a few steps into an ungraded swale, a bit of the shoulder washed out from a rain probably. I stumbled- one step and then another- and then was in free-fall head-first, over the edge of some ravine I couldn't see. Time seemed to slow down: it felt like I was falling into a bottomless pit.

4

Then came the terrible crunch of the impact as I landed on my head. After that, the crack of my ribs, then my legs. When I came to my senses I was lying on my back as though I were in bed. For a moment I thought I might still *be* in bed, in the middle of a nightmare. I didn't know where I was. I didn't usually walk on Hammertown Road, and I didn't remember ever seeing anywhere along the road where a person could fall off the edge of a wall or into some ravine. I didn't know how long I'd been there; it could have been minutes or hours. I was as dizzy as if I'd just stepped off a merry-go-round. I became aware of a warm tickle of blood running down my face. When I reached up to feel my scalp, it felt like my finger went into a hole in my skull.

I knew I was in deep trouble if I didn't get help. I thought to look for my cell phone, which had been in my pocket, but when I checked it was no longer there.

I was hurting all over, and could feel what I thought were jagged rocks poking into my back. I didn't know the extent of my injuries, but I was aware enough to know I was hurt badly. I was a sports coach at the high school and trained in first-aid, and I knew that someone who had hit their head like I had shouldn't be moved.

But I thought: move or die at the bottom of a ditch.

So I decided to try to get to my knees. I had trouble using my left arm; it was awkward trying to lift myself up. I was unprepared for the amount of pain that shot through me when I shifted my body. I fell back onto my side. For my second attempt, I readied myself for the pain. I made it to my knees but could only stay hunched up in a ball.

Now it was gravity's turn. It felt like my entire body was melting into a puddle of pain at my feet. It became clear that it was my upper body that was hurting more than anything else. My legs hurt, but nothing like what I was feeling in my ribs, shoulders, back, neck and head. I almost decided to lie back down, but knew if I did that I probably wouldn't make it up again.

I decided to call out for help. I wasn't sure anyone would hear me. Hammertown Road is a dead-end, and quiet on the busiest of nights; there are only a few houses, and one side of the road is mostly woods and cornfields. But I began to scream: *Help! Please God help me! Could someone help me!* I tried yelling in a variety of ways, as though different arrangements of words might make my cries more intelligible or easier to hear. I have no idea how long I screamed. I'm not even certain I was actually making a sound. It took all I could muster to call out into the night. Each time I yelled my breath became shallower. I had to stop and then gather up my strength to make another try. My shouts became softer and softer until it seemed I was talking to myself. By the time I stopped screaming, I could no longer breathe.

But then a strange sense of peace overcame me, flooding around me as though I were immersed in a warm bath. I was at peace with my pain and the blood that by now had covered my head and I could feel soaking into my shirt and jacket. I felt a profound acceptance of my injuries. I could barely rise to my knees, let alone get up and move to find help. With a contentment that surprised me, I accepted that I was going to die.

They say when you're dying that your life flashes before you, and lying there in the gully I thought of my kids, how they would be without a father. I thought of my parents, my brother and sister, my friends. I thought of my ex-wives. I thought, with disappointment, how I would not be able to go to work on Monday. A great number of things flashed through my mind. And then I thought of Robert.

My wife Yanina and I had not heard from our son Robert in three days. This had happened several times in the past. Our practice was for one of us to stay home with our two youngest kids, and the other to make the trip to Avondale, Arizona, about 1 ½ hours west of our new home in Queen Creek, Arizona, to be sure Robert was okay. Robert was on dialysis, and had struggled over the past six years with kidney disease, but had bravely decided to go to a technical school to study automotive mechanics. He had come with us to Arizona because of his illness, but he was 18 and wanted to be his own man, so, with our approval, he made the decision to live on his own. We were proud of him, but often worried, too. On this day I had been invited to go aboard my friend Bryan's boat, so our two young kids went with my wife to check on Robert. When Yanina got to Robert's apartment she knocked. There was no answer. Since Robert had lost his keys, Yanina had given him her set. So she went to the office to get the keys, and when she opened the door and walked inside, Robert was lying on the kitchen floor.

My wife ran screaming out to the car. She called me. I had just arrived at Bryan's house. All I remember of that moment is getting out of the car at Bryan's home howling, "My son Robert is dead!" Bryan drove me to Avondale. When I arrived at Robert's apartment, it was a crime scene. Since no one had seen Robert for several days, the police pulled me aside to ask me some questions.

To this day, I have never asked my wife to describe the moment she found Robert lying on the kitchen floor. I can only imagine what she must see in her memories.

We were later told Robert had been dead three or four days.

My son Robert died alone in his apartment with no one there to comfort him. I was facing exactly the same fate, lying on the bottom of the gully.

I didn't want to die like my son.

There in the gully, no one would ever think to look for me. I didn't want anyone to find me days later, my body bloated or half-eaten by coyotes, vultures circling overhead. I wanted a decent proper burial. I wanted a wake and a funeral and a memorial service. Of all the things I could have been thinking about at the time, strange as it sounds, lying there at the bottom of that ditch with blood running down my face, pain piercing my body, all I could think about was how I wanted a mortician to patch up my battered body, dress me in a suit, give me a final haircut, and lay me out on view. I could either die in this hole or somehow I could get myself up to the road where someone might find me and give me a proper burial.

And so I decided to climb up out of there. People who later saw the gully I fell into said they were amazed that I could have climbed out, that it must have taken an almost superhuman will-to-live. But I didn't climb up out of that ditch to live. I climbed up, inch by agonizing inch, to die.

2

Stairway
to Heaven

I was light-headed, in great pain, but I decided to try to climb up to the road. I had no idea if I could even move. If I couldn't, I would die right where I was. It was dark but I could see shadows. There was what looked to be a field behind me, and off to my side was a steep stone wall. I thought the road must be at the top of the wall, but that wall looked tall as a skyscraper. I didn't think I could ever get up it.

I started to crawl. There were a number of rocks on the bottom of the gully, and as I crawled slowly over them the rocks dug into my knees. *Keep moving*, I said to myself. Each small movement of my arms forward, each slide of my knees, cost me so much energy, caused so much pain, I felt I couldn't go on. I was having trouble breathing; each time I moved I gasped for air.

Keep moving.

I started to pray. I prayed to God that the direction I was taking was the right one, that I would somehow make it to the road. But one thing I didn't pray for was that I might live: I was in so much pain, and bleeding so much, that I no longer thought living to be an option. There was no longer a fork in the road in front of me like there had always been for all my other decisions in life. There was only one path to take, and that was

9

the path to the road, and then, climbing farther, right up the stairway to Heaven and into God's arms. There wasn't a doubt in my mind that was where I was headed.

After crawling over the rocks, I had moved past the wall and reached what seemed to be the base of a hill. I stayed there a while to catch my breath. The hill was not vertical like the wall, but still very steep. As I knelt there, I wondered how I would reach the top. So far I had moved-slowly, painfully- across level ground. But now I had to climb. I could see the shadowy shapes of trees on the hill, and could feel leaves and twigs under my hands. Until this time I hadn't used my legs to push off, but now I needed to try. At first my feet slipped on the leaves and I fell back. But on my next try I got some traction and began to climb. At times I fell to my belly and tried to slither forward, inch by inch.

Partway up I didn't think I could go on. I lay there for a time. I could feel Death with me on that embankment. I felt terribly alone, and yet in the fullness of that time many people came to see me in my mind- my family and friends and children.

When I was a small boy, my great grandfather, Robert Baker, looked after me every morning while my mom and dad were at work and my sister and brother were in school. I remember well my last day of Kindergarten. I woke up to some wonderful smells in the kitchen. Grandpa, as we called him, had made breakfast- eggs, pancakes, bacon. Then we watched my favorite shows on TV- Captain Kangaroo, Mister Rogers, Batman.

"Time to catch the bus, Jimmy."

So after washing up we walked down to the end of the driveway and waited for the bus. Fifteen minutes. Thirty minutes. No bus.

"Jimmy, you stay right here by this tree and don't move unless the bus comes along. Then you tell the driver to honk his horn and wait for me."

I did as I was told while Grandpa walked back to the house. Still no bus. When Grandpa returned some minutes later, he said, "Jimmy,

I called your mom. We were having so much fun eating breakfast and watching television that we missed the bus."

We waited until after lunch when my mom came home and drove me to school. I showed up at school with only about one hour left in the day, and when I told my teacher and classmates why I was late, what my Grandpa had done for me to celebrate making it through my first year of school, I was King for a very short day.

My great grandfather died when I was eleven years old, in 1976; that was my first experience of death. As a lay there halfway up that embankment, I couldn't help but think that my children Logan and Lauryn had already experienced the deaths of several loved ones by the time they were that age, and that now, added to those, would be their father.

I didn't yell out any more. Since I was going to die, I didn't see the need. But there was this consolation: I thought how if I died there, I would at least be going to see my two boys, Robert and James, in Heaven. They, too, had already come to see me as I lay there in that ravine. There was a hotness and wetness on my face, and I could no longer tell what was blood and what was tears.

After my first wife and I had divorced, I was back living with my folks until I could get on my feet again. A very attractive dark-skinned woman had moved just across the street with her two little boys. I thought I would like to get to know her.

My niece Jenesis had become friends with the two little boys, Jon and Robert. Whenever I saw the three kids together, Jenesis would say "Hi, Uncle Jim," and in unison Jon and Robert would say, "Hi, Uncle Jim." Through the grapevine I found out the woman's name was Yanina, though I wasn't sure how to pronounce it. Yanina often sat out on her front porch listening to Spanish music with a friend. When I heard the music I would sit on my parent's front porch so Yanina could see me. I don't think I had ever sat on that porch in my life until I started hearing Yanina's music. Months passed, and I couldn't help but notice Yanina's foot-high lawn. I'm a landscaper, so an uncut lawn has always bothered me. My parents told me

11

Yanina's mower had broken down, that I should go over and help her fix it. And by the way, they said with a wink, maybe you'll get to know her. I somehow overcame my chronic shyness and walked over.

"Need help fixing your mower?" Probably one of the worst come-on lines in world history, but I had to say something.

"You can try if you want to."

I helped her with her mower, and invited her to go dancing any Friday or Saturday night. At that time in my life, I loved dancing. I usually went every weekend. Usually alone.

Months passed and Yanina hadn't taken me up on my offer. I was busy at work, and rarely saw her. It seemed I would be adding her to my list of unrequited loves. But then one Saturday I answered a knock at my door.

Yanina. "What are you doing tonight?" she asked.

"You know where I always go on Saturday nights."

"Would it be all right for me to come along?"

"I thought you'd never ask."

We went to the dance club together. I thought we were going as friends, and was prepared for her to dance with whomever she wanted. But as we walked in, she put her arm through mine.

Soon after, I more formally met her boys. While their mother was busy in the kitchen, Jon and Robert led me into their room. I was as nervous as if it were a job interview. In a way, I guess maybe it was. We talked and played some computer games. After that, we walked out into the yard. With Jon and Jenesis on one team, and me and Robert on the other, we played a wiffle ball game that lasted more than 30 innings.

Yanina and I started dating, and our son Logan was born on August 23, 1997. I was privileged to be present at the birth. As the baby was lifted up into the arms of the midwife, I was sure I saw a penis. But our midwife said, "Congratulations, you have a beautiful baby girl." I knew very well this was the first birth I had ever witnessed, but besides being male myself, I had been in enough boy's locker rooms over the years playing and coaching football and basketball and track, that I knew a penis when I saw one. The midwife turned the baby over and said, sheepishly, "Oh, I'm sorry, you have a beautiful baby boy! Congratulations!"

Soon after, on September 20, 1997, Yanina and I were married. Not only had we had a child out of wedlock, but I was white and Yanina was a black Spanish girl from Guatemala. But our wedding was not the small-town scandal it might have been. There were whispers and arched eyebrows, but more people welcomed us than not.

Within a year I had gone from being single to married with three kids. It was quite an adjustment. We helped pay for most of our wedding, so funds for a honeymoon were tight. To give ourselves a little alone-time, we ended up going to one of Yanina's friend's houses. It was Halloween, and after Yanina's friends left to give us some privacy, trick-or-treaters started knocking. So Yanina and I spent our honeymoon passing out Halloween candy.

We moved to a little cottage without running water that we got in a foreclosure sale. The boys were happy to have their own rooms, even though Jon's room had no door and Robert had to walk through Jon's room to reach his own. Robert's room was the size of a closet, but at least he could call it his own. I often sat in the living room watching television with baby Logan on my lap.

From the beginning, Jon and Robert called me Jimmy, and that was okay with me. But once, a year or so after the marriage, I went to pick the boys up from an after-school event. I had just arrived and was standing around the corner in the hall, when I overheard another parent asking them if they needed a ride home.

"No," they both said. "Our dad is coming to get us."

Any man can be a father. But to have Jon and Robert call me 'Dad' was one of the greatest compliments of my life.

Hundreds of memories like those were swirling in my mind. Was this what it was like, your life flashing before your eyes as you were about to die? I felt comforted by these memories, but also saddened that I would be leaving it all behind- my children, my family and friends.

My life.

I needed to reach the road. I started to crawl again.

13

I have no idea how long it took me to crawl up that embankment, every inch of my body screaming in pain. But eventually the hillside leveled out. On the roadside I came to a log. I held onto that log as though I were a drowning man clutching the side of a boat. I thought: *my time on earth is done*. I didn't think I could move another muscle. I could hardly breathe. I could feel blood pooling around me on the ground.

Though I'd had a lot of heartache in my life, I felt profoundly grateful. If given the chance, I felt I would do it all again. I remember feeling sorry for the person who would find me on the side of Hammertown Road, probably the next morning, maybe someone out walking their dog or just driving by on their way to work.

And I remember thinking: I still hold our high school track and field record for the hammer-throw. I made the Dean's List a few times, got straight A's my last year in college, finished with a 3.76 GPA, had a successful junior-varsity basketball coaching career, had two wonderful stepchildren and three biological children, got married twice, was part of a successful landscaping business. All things I'm proud of. But this, climbing up out of a pit and hanging onto a log on the side of Hammertown Road, this will be the last thing I will ever succeed at doing. I made it. Someone will see me now, I will be found, and I will be buried.

3
The Light

When I reached the side of the road I was in so much pain, and so tired from the climb up out of that gully, that I closed my eyes and laid there for a time. I closed my eyes partly from pain, partly from exhaustion, partly due to blood and sweat and tears, but also because I didn't want someone to find me dead on the side of the road with my lifeless eyes staring off into nothingness. With some relief, I thought the terrible pain wracking my body would finally cease when I died. It would be better if my eyes were closed.

I had reached the road. There was nothing more I could do.

I was not without fear, or doubt. I believed I would be joining my sons, Robert and James, in Heaven. But how could I know? Maybe death was not what I believed it to be. Maybe, despite everything I hoped, there was no Heaven. Maybe there would be no peace, no rest. My faith was not unshakeable. There had been enough tragedies and terrible struggles in my life to make me wonder. Though I believed in God, and in Heaven, I was not a practicing Christian; I rarely went to church; I didn't know the Bible. I was not at all sure where I stood with God. And so though I accepted my fate, it was not without some dread.

As I lay there in a pool of blood on the side of Hammertown Road, behind my closed eyelids it seemed to be getting lighter, as though I were a child and my mother had turned on the lights in my room to wake me up.

I thought a car might be approaching, the glare from its headlights washing over me. And so I opened my eyes. But I didn't see or hear any cars. Maybe I was hallucinating from loss of blood. Or maybe it was the moon peering out from behind clouds, or the stars in my ringing head, or maybe even someone shining a flashlight in my eyes. The light was coming from above me. I tried to lift my head but the pain was too great. But I was able to roll my body to the right a little and turn my head slightly to look up. All the while the light was growing brighter, shining down on me like a spotlight. The light seemed to be spreading out across the fields and hills like a sunrise.

The light became so intense it was blinding, a brilliant white, but there was also a softness to the light; it felt comforting, as though the light were somehow holding me in its arms. It was the most beautiful thing I had ever seen.

And then, from the midst of the brilliance, a human figure walked toward me. A wind began swirling around me, moving over me and rustling through the trees. My pain subsided. My breathing became much easier.

As my eyes adjusted I could better see the figure in the light: grandfatherly, bearded, wearing what seemed to be a robe, a weathered but kindly face.

Then the light around the figure began to sparkle in a variety colors, a kaleidoscope of twinkling stars, a frame around the white light at the center where the figure stood. And there, standing behind and to one side of the figure, I saw my two sons who had passed away, Robert and James. They no longer looked sickly.

I remembered then that one of the things I had yelled down in the hole was, "Please God, help me!" Though I had fallen into a gully and landed on my head, though I had lost a great amount of blood, though it was possible I was delirious and in shock, I knew, without a doubt in my mind, to the depths of my very soul, that the figure standing before me was God.

He had come to take me to Heaven. Though I was heartbroken that I would be leaving my children and family, my life, I was as ready as a person could be to die.

"I'm ready to come with You to Heaven, God, if You want me."

Maybe I spoke these words, maybe I thought them. I'm not sure. But God heard them.

The wind ceased and a great stillness and hush settled over me. God spoke, not from the midst of fire, not like thunder, or the sound of many waves, or a voice that stripped bare the forests, like in scripture. More a reassuring and comforting voice that blossomed inside my soul, from within, rather than from without.

God told me it was not my time, that there were things for me to do for Him on earth.

"But I'm just Jim Bay, an ordinary man. There's nothing special about me."

God told me we are all special because we are all His children, as was Jesus, and that He was here for everyone and everything. Most important was to believe, to have faith, and to pray. He had heard me saying the Prayer of Jabez and asking for blessings. For everyone who asks, God has blessings.

"I've always believed in You, but I've always doubted the Bible. People have always killed in the name of the Bible."

God told me that those in power interpret His words for their own benefit, to keep themselves in control. But did I notice that in the end they always fall from control forever?

"But what about someone like me, someone who doesn't know the Bible. And many people cannot read at all. Many people don't know the Bible."

God told me that one does not need to know the Bible to know Him.

"What can *I* do?"

God told me we take the things He created for granted, that we must learn to appreciate the blessings that are in everything. He told me *I* must appreciate the blessings that are in everything. He told me to share the events of this night with all who would listen. He said He would be communicating with me in many ways, and that I would understand better in time why it was not my time to come to Heaven. I was to be alert and listen for His messages.

God turned and began moving away, and again the wind came and swirled around me and through the trees. Robert and James followed God into the distance. As God left, the circle of light that had flooded the area faded with each step, until it looked as if He was walking away holding a candle. As the light faded to a small point the dark began to fold over me. And then all was again darkness.

The wind stopped.

And then the pain returned, white-hot swords piercing my body. My breathing became labored. Again I noticed the trickle of blood across my face. I had been so focused on God that all this had faded for a time into the background. I was again in the still dark, alone, clutching a log on the side of Hammertown Road.

But I was not alone. Though I could no longer see God or the Light, I knew I had not been abandoned. I was trembling, in awe of the experience I had just had. I had climbed up out of that ditch to die, but God had come to me in my time of need and told me I would live. I would again see my family, my children. There was work for me to do in the world. I didn't doubt anything God had told me, but I didn't know how to do what God had asked of me. He had given me no guidance or instructions on what to do next. Though my body was broken, my spirit was not. I felt refreshed, as after a good night's sleep. I had been uplifted. I knew I had to try.

From where I lay on the side of the road, through the blood dripping into my eyes, I saw a house with its lights on. I knew that was where I must go. But *how* was the question. And so though I was not at all sure I could do it, I got up and started to walk toward that house. Toward the light.

In August 2005, after 40 years of living in New York State's Hudson Valley, my wife and I packed up our family and moved to Phoenix, Arizona. As we unpacked I came across a book titled The Prayer of Jabez *by Dr. Bruce Wilkinson. I didn't put the book in that box; I'd never seen it or heard of it in my life. My wife had never seen it. I didn't buy this book. My wife did not buy it. To this day I don't know where it came from.*

The titular prayer, from 1 Chronicles 4:10, is this: "And Jabez called on the God of Israel, saying, 'Oh that You would bless me indeed, and enlarge my territory, that Your hand would be with me, and that You would keep me from evil, that I may not cause pain.' So God granted him what he requested."

When I moved to Arizona I was unemployed. It was the first time in my adult life that I didn't have a job, and I was struggling mightily with that, especially since I had a wife and children to support. My anxiety was so bad that I couldn't relax at all during the week; I spent all my time looking for work.

Instead of throwing that book away, or placing it unread on a shelf, I read it, and it gave me some hope and helped me feel better about myself. The Prayer told me that if you asked, God would answer- "So God granted him what he requested." It comforted me to think that maybe, just maybe, God would give me what I asked for.

It changed the way I prayed. I had never prayed every day. Like many people, I prayed only when I wanted something done for someone I loved or knew, or when I needed something myself. But after reading the book I began to pray faithfully every day. I would recite the Prayer of Jabez, and then say my own prayer, asking for blessings for myself and others. I asked God to do his work through me. I repeated the Prayer of Jabez when I awoke in the morning and again before going to sleep.

If there is one thing I've learned in this life, it's that the old adage, Be careful what you ask for, *is one of the truest things ever said. I would have been satisfied with a new job, with my kids doing well in school. I would have been happy with losing some weight. I could have used a new car. But God had other ideas. He had me fall into a gully and shatter my body. He decided to appear to me to tell me I had things to do in this world. He told me He had heard my prayers. I asked God for something, and He gave me something, all right. It wasn't even close to what I thought it would be.*

They say if you want fruit sometimes you need to shake the tree. Maybe all along, all through my life, God was giving me signs, or speaking to me in a still voice. Maybe I was so busy, like we all are, working and paying bills and raising a family and watching television, that I never noticed. Maybe God decided with me he needed to be a little more drastic.

4

You'll Never Walk Alone

I hoped that angels would come, one on each arm, and lift me up and fly me to that house. But no angels came. There was only me and my agony in the quiet and dark on the side of the road. God had not sent angels to uplift my body, but He had uplifted my spirit. My body was shattered, but my spirit was not. God had given me hope that I might again see my children and family and friends. And God gave me the Light, though now it was only a house light in the darkness to walk toward.

If I was going to reach that light, it was up to me. From where I was lying, I realized I had two options: either I could crawl, or I could get up and walk. Given the amount of pain I had felt simply trying to crawl, I doubted I could walk. But I decided to try. The thought of crawling all the way to that house- the time it would take and the blood I would lose along the way- decided it for me. Before I tried to stand, I knew to brace myself for more pain. But I had no idea just how much more pain there was going to be. I was able to push off the log with my right arm and get back to my knees. I then managed to stand halfway up, but I couldn't take the pain and fell back to my knees.

I'll have to crawl.

But I gave it one more try and rose into a slouch. That is more or less the way I stayed. I couldn't stand upright. When I stood I was so dizzy I almost fell over backwards. And now that I was standing, the blood that was seeping from my head wound only had one way to flow, and that was down and into my face. I started walking, or rather shuffling, dragging my leaden feet inch by inch, as though my ankles were locked to a ball and chain. I almost gave up after my first step. The pain I experienced at the bottom of the culvert was bad, as was the pain when I climbed up the embankment. But the pain from trying to walk was even worse. Each time I touched a foot to the ground, white-hot vibrations shot through me, all through my body. I was so dizzy I felt like I could collapse at any moment. I took breaks to catch my breath, crouching down with my hands on my knees. I knew if I slipped to my knees I wouldn't be able to get up again.

I prayed that someone would be home at the house.

I felt like a tottering infant taking baby steps. Every step I took it seemed like the house took two steps backwards. I knew from how light-headed I was, and from the blood still running down my face, that I had to get to that house.

Get to the door, just get to the door.

Once I reached the lawn I recognized the house as my neighbor's. The walk became more difficult. I was barely able to lift my feet off the ground, and now I was walking through grass, which was harder to move my feet through, and the lawn also sloped up to the front door, so I was walking a little uphill. I still didn't know whether anyone was home; there was only a dim light coming through one of the windows. But I reached the door and knocked. I had never knocked on her door before. After some minutes, the porch light came on, flooding around me nearly as brightly as God's Light.

Having reached the house, I felt like a guy who had the first five numbers in the lottery, and when the door opened, that was the sixth, the jackpot. I don't remember doing it, but my neighbor told me later that when she answered the door I asked, "Can you call 911?"

22

Porch Light

I had just returned home after a 4-hour drive from visiting my relatives in New Jersey. I was doing my usual routine- unpacking, making my lunch for work the next day, getting ready to shower- while listening to music on my radio, loud enough so I can hear it wherever I am in the house, upstairs or downstairs. Listening to music always puts me in a good mood.

I noticed that the radio was playing two stations at once. I don't know why that happens, but it does sometimes, maybe because of the weather. The song that was playing was clear enough, but in the background I could hear a faint talking. I walked over to the stereo, and was just about to change the dial to another station, when I heard a voice again. It sounded like it was coming from the stereo speaker next to the stairs going down to the basement. So I stood next to that speaker and sure enough I heard it again. But this time I could make out a word.

It sounded like, "help."

Then again- help!- but this time it seemed to be coming from the front door. I walked over to the door, turned on the porch light. I don't remember if I peeked out of the side windows to see if there was someone there, but I opened the door anyway. And there, standing before me, was a man, dressed in what looked like gym clothes, covered with blood. Blood was streaming down his face. He looked like someone out of a horror movie. I was frightened; maybe I shouldn't have opened the door.

I don't remember who spoke first, but the man told me he was my next-door neighbor, Jim, and then, despite all that blood, I recognized him. I asked him what happened and he started to tell me about his fall on the road, but he was talking fast and I wasn't able to understand exactly what he meant and where he fell. I turned around and ran up the stairs to grab the telephone to call 911. As I was talking to the dispatcher, I went back to the front door and saw that Jim had collapsed on the front lawn. While the dispatcher was asking me for my name, my address, and details of what happened, Jim *was still talking with me from where he was laid out on the ground, trying his best to explain. As I was trying to relay the information to the dispatcher, I saw in the light from my porch that there was a very big gash on Jim's head. When I told the dispatcher this, he told me to find a towel and hold it against the gash, which I did. Jim was moaning, I think about the pain in his back.*

After I hung up, Jim asked me to contact his brother. In all that pain, with all that blood, somehow, he was able to give me the phone number. I called, but I think it was the business number. It rang and then went to voicemail. When I told Jim this, he gave me another number and said to talk over the voicemail, because they would hear me. I did that and then someone picked up. It was Jim's brother, I believe, and I told him who I was, and that Jim was in my front yard, badly hurt, and bleeding profusely.

An ambulance came down Hammertown Road and passed right by the house. So when they turned around, I started to flicker the porch light on and off so they would realize where to stop. Soon after that, the police came, along with a fire truck and another ambulance. I couldn't remember another time there were so many people on my quiet street. I still didn't see anyone who looked like a relative. Just then the flood lights from the fire truck lit up the entire yard.

And then I could clearly see the blood in splotches and smears all over the grass.

The paramedics were asking Jim questions and trying to help him. They had cut open his jacket so they could give him aid. The medics kept walking quickly between their vehicles for supplies and then back to Jim. They were starting to bandage him up, put his neck in a brace, trying to calm him down. I think they started an IV on him right there on the lawn, too.

The police officer was asking me questions about what happened, how I found Jim, what he had said. I gave him all the information I could, which I'm afraid wasn't very much. I didn't know Jim had fallen in the culvert down the street from my house. I thought he had somehow fallen in the road, and was wondering how he could possibly have so much damage to his body. Jim's MP3 player was on the ground and I picked it up and gave it to the officer so that it didn't get lost or stepped on.

At some point, Jim's brother came over, along with Jim's parents. I don't recall speaking with them too long, as they were very concerned about Jim and standing close to him.

I had no idea what else was wrong with Jim, besides the back pain and the gash in his head, but I guessed it was very serious, as the medics didn't move him for quite some time. When they did try to move him onto a stretcher, Jim screamed in pain. I think they wanted to fly him by helicopter to a hospital in Poughkeepsie, but it was by then too foggy, so Jim was loaded into the ambulance.

After the ambulance left my property, the paramedics came over and picked up all their supplies and even took a bucket of water and washed all the blood off the lawn. I thought that was good of them. I don't know what time everyone finally left my house, but I remember that I didn't sleep much that night, recalling all that had happened. A few days later, when I heard that Jim could have died out there on Hammertown Road, I felt such a sense of gratitude that I had returned home that night. If I had stayed in New Jersey any longer, Jim might have collapsed or bled to death, or gone into a coma and died all alone in that culvert.

I still play the stereo really loud, but now I peek out some of the windows once in awhile to see what's going on out there. And every night, I leave my porch light on.

    -Indira Velasquez

I passed out on my neighbor's lawn. I don't know how long I was out, but when I woke up, the lawn was lit up with lights from the fire truck and police cars. There were a great number of people on the lawn. Not long ago I had thought I might die alone, but now I was surrounded by people.

I was now in the hands of others. I had thought reaching the log on the side of the road would be my last accomplishment, but somehow, with all the pain and loss of blood, I had walked to my neighbor's house. I had done all I could do.

I heard someone say, "We have a head injury here. We have a deformity of the left shoulder."

Who Would Have Looked for Him There?

On November 15, 2009, I was on routine patrol with a new recruit. At about 9:30 p.m., the Dutchess County 911 dispatcher announced a rescue squad call in Pine Plains on the 911 Police channel. They generally announce fire and rescue calls so that the police in the area know when there's a call. The call was for a man who had fallen down an embankment of some kind and was injured on Hammertown Road. It was a relatively slow night, and so even though I was two towns away, since I had a recruit with me, I figured I'd head that way. I remember the drive being a little foggy, so it took a while to get there.

When we arrived, the Pine Plains Fire Department and rescue squad, as well as a Pine Plains Police Officer, were on scene and assisting the patient. They were in the front yard of someone's home. I didn't know the woman in the front doorway. I stood off to the side and watched and waited to see if my assistance would be needed. I didn't get close enough to the victim at that point to know who he was, but I noticed he was obviously in a lot of pain. There was a significant amount of blood and he screamed every time the EMT's touched him. I kept thinking to myself, this guy fell down an embankment? I'm somewhat familiar with the surrounding area. I looked around and thought about the landscape. I couldn't recall there being any deep drop-offs nearby. Where had this guy fallen?

I was only there a few minutes when I saw my cousin John walking up to the scene. He owns the house next door and runs a landscaping business headquartered next to that. I walked over to him. He saw me but didn't stop walking. As he passed by me he said, "It's Jimmy." The man laid out on the lawn was my cousin Jimmy.

I started thinking more about what I was seeing. I knew Jimmy liked to walk a lot. In fact, I remembered seeing him walking all the time. Then I went over and started asking him questions. "Jimmy, what happened? Did you get hit by a car? Was there a car involved?" He was still conscious at this point, and he told me no, he just fell. Then I noticed my aunt and uncle were there. I started asking them questions too, but they didn't know anything more.

Eventually, the EMTs had Jim on the stretcher and ready to go to the hospital. Usually this would not be a police matter, and since this wasn't my call, once the victim is transported, I would ordinarily leave, too. But this was my cousin and I was not satisfied with Jimmy's answers to my questions. I told my recruit that we had to find where Jimmy fell because this just didn't add up. He fell off the road? How could he be hurt so badly? I figured if he had fallen somewhere between the two houses, he would go to his house, not his neighbor's. So we started walking west, looking along both sides of the road. About a hundred feet down the road, we started seeing blood spattered along the shoulder. We followed that a little way farther and found a spot where he must have stopped for a short time because there was considerably more blood pooled there. It struck me as almost horrific that I was following my cousin Jimmy's blood trail. And that's when, in the beam from our flashlights, I saw it. The leaves were disturbed and there was more blood. I walked closer and couldn't believe my eyes. There, right alongside the road, was a sharp drop-off straight down where a drainage pipe runs under the road. I looked over the edge. It was at least fifteen feet straight down and nothing but jagged rocks. Shining my flashlight into the gully, I saw Jimmy's cell phone down there and a lot more blood. Now I knew why he was in so much pain.

While my recruit climbed down to retrieve Jimmy's cell phone, I immediately called the 911 dispatcher on my radio to advise them of what I had found. I felt it was extremely important for the EMTs and doctors to know exactly what they were dealing with. It would make a difference in how they would treat Jimmy and where they would bring him. I then went and found John, who was preparing to go to the hospital with his parents, and told him what had happened and where Jimmy had fallen.

Later, I drove to the fire house in town to see my sister. She's an EMT but she had been out on another call that night. We talked about Jimmy for a few minutes and I went back to work. It was hard to think about much else that evening, but luckily it stayed a slow night. My sister told me the next day that Jimmy had broken most of his body, including his skull. I couldn't believe that he was able to crawl out of that ditch and all the way to his neighbor's house. He surely would have died in that hole if he didn't get out. Who would have looked for him there?

Rich Brenner
Deputy Sheriff
Dutchess County Sheriff's Office

AND YOU
HEALED ME

Patient: Bay, James

St. Francis Hospital in Poughkeepsie is around 25 miles from my house. I don't remember much about the ambulance ride. But I do remember the pain. God had promised me I was going to live, but I was in so much pain I felt like I was dying. At one point I remember the paramedic saying, "I'm with you. I'll get you there." The driver, a woman, said, "What about me? I'm driving. Don't I have anything to do with this?" I don't know if they were kidding, but if it didn't hurt so damn much I would have laughed.

I remember the wheels of the gurney hitting the pavement outside the ambulance. As I was being wheeled into the ER I have vague memories of someone saying, "Good job, James" and being shifted from one gurney to the next. I remember passing by people in the hallway. The fluorescent lights flashing by overhead looked nothing like God's Light, and I hoped God was still with me.

CHIEF COMPLAINT: Trauma Code 99.
ADMITTING DIAGNOSIS: CAT scan of the head showed a 2 millimeter left subdural, there is a coronal suture diastasis with possible left fragmentation, no evidence of depression. CAT scan of the cervical spine shows a C7 pedicle fracture, left C7 pilar fracture, CAT scan of the thoracic spine has fractures of

T10, T12, and T6, and a costal process fracture of T2 through 4, T6 through 10. CAT scan of the chest showed rib fractures, the right 1, 2, 3 and 8 and on the left 2 though 6, 10, 11 with a small hemothorax bilaterally, pulmonary contusion, left scapular fracture, large scalp flap laceration, acute pain due to trauma.

PLAN: The patient will be admitted and he will remain in cervical collar, scalp laceration cleaned and irrigated, sutured. Cranial and cervical injuries reviewed and the patient will have repeat CAT scan in the Intensive Care Unit. Continue cervical collar, repeat CAT scan in AM and also cervical spine and thoracic spine precautions, acute pain management, follow-up hemoglobin and hemocrit.

I was admitted to the hospital on Sunday night. I kept the doctors busy: a vena cava filter to protect against a pulmonary embolism; X-rays of just about my entire body; CAT scans; feeding tubes and breathing tubes and mechanical ventilation; blood test after blood test; neurological and lab tests. The 'large scalp flap laceration' turned out to be 4.7 inches. The doctors sutured my scalp, and I received a blood transfusion since I had lost so much blood.

I had broken 23 bones, with 26 fractures, including 11 ribs, 10 vertebrae- including 3 in two places- my left shoulder and my skull.

From the Caring Bridge website- Background Story:
Jim has been walking almost every day since last Fall in order to help him lose weight. In some rough notes of calculations kept: Jim has walked over 1,000 miles since then. Because of family history of being overweight, over the summer, in early August, Jim's brother John started to walk with Jim. Jim & John stared to have walking "business meetings". Their average "meeting" time was 85 minutes of brisk walking. As you can tell, this accident is a total shock to us and the family. No matter what weather it was outside, Jim walked so much that this accident just doesn't make any sense. At this point we're investigating what might have happened because Jim still

doesn't have a memory of what happened. Once we know anything we'll pass it on. Thanks to all of you who have written to Jim.
  Love, John and Mary Ann Bay

Due to my head trauma, to decrease pressure in my brain and to prevent further swelling, and because of the intense pain from all my broken bones, on Monday night the doctors induced a coma. What I remember of the following week are the vivid dreams- psychedelic IMAX high-definition surround-sound. There was one dream that kept recurring. I was walking down a road toward a cornfield. The corn was like you see it in the autumn, golden-brown and brittle. In a ticket booth on the edge of the cornfield sat a scarecrow. He didn't look much like the scarecrow from the *Wizard of Oz*: he had malevolent eyes, a red hat, and ripped-up flannel clothing. He had a very human mouth. His name was Sam. We talked about a great many things: how wonderful it is to walk in nature; about politics- it was Sam's view that the federal government was too damn big for its own good, that the country was too big to manage, and he suggested we should start over again; about sports- every time I saw Sam he would give me some of the scores from that day. Sam told me he had kids of his own, one boy and one girl. It was his job to sit in that booth on the edge of that cornfield. Always, after our talks, we said, "See you tomorrow." I made this walk to see Sam many times, each time healthy- no broken bones, no gash in my head. Every time I went to see Sam the weather was different: one trip it was sunny; another trip it was cloudy.

Even today, years after my accident, I continue to have very vivid dreams. But I've only seen Sam one more time since my stay in the hospital. One night, after I put my head down on the pillow, I packed a lunch, left my house, drove to the cornfield, brought Sam some food, and it was just like old times, talking about nature and politics and trades in sports.

People ask me: What's it like to be in a coma? When she hit her head, Dorothy went to Oz. I have absolutely no idea where I went.

***

33

When I was still in the coma I had a visitor at my bedside. I didn't recognize her. She was dressed in white. Her voice was calm, reassuring. She told me that God had come to me for a reason and that I would learn in time what that reason was. She said I would learn what I should be doing with my life. She said not to be afraid, that I was in good hands. And as suddenly as she had arrived, she was gone.

I was in a coma for seven days. If you've ever been under anesthesia, you know how it is waking up: it feels like you're pulling yourself out of quicksand. Coming out of my coma, I had that not-quite-all-here groggy feeling for many days. I knew I was in a hospital but I didn't know which one. I didn't know how long I'd been in the hospital: it could have been days; it could have been weeks; I was hoping it hadn't been years. I was always thirsty, due in part to the feeding and breathing tubes down my throat. I remember fantasizing or dreaming about the Kool-Aid guy, that mascot from television commercials, bursting through my hospital wall and pouring me a tall cool glass. I remember hearing snatches of a conversation about how I could die from pneumonia. I recall having a rash from an allergic reaction to an antibiotic, and getting my stomach pumped when I got sick from my liquid diet. I had a breathing tube so I couldn't speak, and I remember being hot, looking at the fan in the room and twirling my eyes round and round. My Aunt Barbara, figuring out my meaning, said, "He wants the fan on!" I remember hearing the medivac helicopter- I was in the trauma unit and that helicopter rattled the walls each time it took off- and feeling somewhat forlorn each time I heard it, knowing that there was someone at that very moment who was hurt as badly as I was. Whenever I heard the *click clack* or squeak of shoes on the hallway tiles, I wanted desperately to get out of bed and walk. I remember peeing and expecting to feel something warm dribbling down my legs; it took me a while to figure out I had a catheter. I have the clearest memory of one nurse, who had given me an enema, saying cheerily, "Good, Jim, good, good, good." God bless nurses. All of this was slowly coming into consciousness.

Coming back to me, too, were memories of that night: my fall, crying out for help, my climb up the embankment, the walk to my neighbor's

34

house, the crack of my skull as I hit the rocks, the blood and pain. Every cell in my body seemed to remember the pain. But I also remembered the Light. And I remembered God.

In my hospital bed, I had all the time in the world to think about that night, and for a time I doubted that what I had experienced was real. After all, I *did* land on my head. Maybe I was only hallucinating; maybe the pain was so great that I only saw what I wanted to see; maybe it was only a drug-induced dream during my coma. But I remembered how other momentous events in my life- the births of my children, my weddings, a move cross-country to Arizona, graduation from high school and college- could also seem like dreams. I would wake up the next morning wondering, 'Did that really happen?' And then I'd hear the baby crying or feel my wife beside me in bed or see the diploma in a frame on the wall, and I'd know it was no dream. And so it was with God. I could still feel vividly that God was with me. The Light was there, more real than a memory. It seemed to have burned itself into my retinas, shimmering there behind my closed eyelids, and after I opened my eyes the Light washed everything with brightness. The voice of God was there too, still whispering to me, telling me that I had work to do in the world, that it was not my time to come to Heaven. I knew others would doubt, but there was not a doubt in my mind that God had come to me in my time of need. And there was not a doubt in my mind that I would do what God had asked me to do. I would tell others the story of that night.

After I was awake, the nurses and doctors gave me a pad and pen so I could write my requests. In elementary school, Kindergarten through 6th, I always got D's in Handwriting. In 4th Grade, I got A's in all subjects- except for Handwriting. But on my report card for the third quarter, my teacher, Mrs. Ackerman, felt so bad for me that she gave me an A in Handwriting simply so I could experience straight A's. Next quarter I was back to a D, but I will never forget what she did for me. And so my handwriting- chicken-scratch at the best of times- was apparently so illegible- "It looks like hieroglyphics" I heard one of the nurses say- that the effort was soon abandoned.

***

Soon after I arrived at the hospital, my hands were so swollen from all the needle pricks they were giving me to draw blood that they couldn't get a good IV in me, so they used a Picc line instead. It was placed in my upper chest, on the right side. It worked well until one night a nurse realized it was getting infected. The nurse said it would have to be pulled out and a regular IV started. After four different nurses and fourteen attempts, they still couldn't get an IV in me that would flow properly. In desperation, they called in the nurse with the reputation for getting IVs in any patient. I expected a brute of a woman, an East German steroid-pumped weight-lifter type, but the nurse who came in was a petite elderly woman, almost grandmotherly; you could tell she had a lot of experience. But even she took three stabs before sinking one in me. I'm sure I wanted to laugh, but with all my broken ribs I kept my mouth shut. The next day the IV fell out and everyone decided to keep it out.

There were times during those days when I wasn't sure I would ever get out of the hospital. But one thing I knew for sure: I didn't want to die there, under fluorescent lights, with that god-awful hospital smell in my nostrils. I thought of my son James.

A few years after our son Logan was born, Yanina and I decided to try for another baby. My wife became pregnant and, based on all the ultrasounds and gynecological tests, the pregnancy was progressing well. On the night of May 29, 2000, around 11:00, after I had gone to bed, I woke to my wife screaming in pain in the living room. Like all fathers, I imagine I bounced off the walls and tripped over my own feet as I hurriedly tried to pack a suitcase. We drove to the hospital with Yanina in the backseat. I know in movies panicked fathers drive 100 miles per hour, weaving through traffic, but I more or less drove the speed limit the entire way. I guess I thought if we were stopped it would make the trip even longer.

When we arrived at the hospital Yanina was ten centimeters dilated. She was ready to deliver. It was time for an emergency C-section.

I dressed in scrubs so I could be in the operating room. While dressing in the locker room area, the doctor and gynecologist told me, since Yanina was only 23 ½ weeks pregnant, that our baby had only a fifty percent chance of living. I never thought I would hear words like those. Those words might have been the prongs of a Taser shot directly into my chest. My stomach was in knots, but I quickly realized I needed to be strong for Yanina and our baby. It was a good thing I was wearing a surgical mask to hide my quivering lip.

The baby was so small the doctors had trouble locating him, but on May 30, 2000, at 2:54 AM, our baby son was born, weighing one pound four ounces. The doctors swept him up and did what they needed to do and got him into an incubator for a ride to another hospital. Yanina was brought back to her room. Before our little son was transported they wheeled him into our room so we could get a look at him.

I stayed with my wife for a while and made calls to her family and to mine. In the hospital room, Yanina and I discussed a name for our boy. Because we were still so early in the pregnancy, we hadn't discussed it yet. We settled quickly on James. But we were not sure about a middle name. We each suggested a few options, and then Yanina thought of Ulysses. And so, like the mythical Greek hero, our son James was given the name Ulysses to give him the strength he would need for the battles in the days and weeks ahead.

After I left the hospital I went home to tell our three sons Robert, Jon and Logan, that they had a brother named James. My family was now in three places- Yanina in one hospital, James Ulysses in another, and my sons at home. I told my boys that baby James might not live. After getting some help to care for my boys, I was off to the neonatal care unit of the hospital to be with my baby son.

The first time I saw little James in the hospital I was overwhelmed. He was hooked up to more monitors and tubes than I thought his little body could bear. His spot in the room was 1-9. He was only 23 ½ weeks, but he had quite a mane of hair. He also had all his toes and fingers. I suppose all parents look at those and count, just to be sure. The only thing I couldn't see was the color of his eyes; his eyelids weren't open yet.

37

I stayed a long time that day. The doctors and nurses were all very kind and professional, explaining what each machine was for and what each beep and hum from the machines meant. I met other parents that day whose babies were there too. It was then, looking at my little boy in his incubator, his chest rising and falling, his little arms and legs flailing around, there in a bright room full of other babies fighting for their lives, that I realized profoundly what a miracle it is to have a healthy baby. There is so much that can go wrong.

I guess maybe even then I had a hunch what the future held. Despite his heroic name, I wasn't sure my little son would ever have the strength to leave the hospital.

Guestbook

That night was like any other; packing lunch for work the next day, getting ready for bed. But, unlike other nights, this one I will forever remember vividly. My mom yelled to my husband Chris and me from the bottom of the stairs. I could hear the panic in her voice, and then my phone started ringing. It was my grandmother. I couldn't understand what she was saying. Something about Uncle Jimmy falling- lots of blood, close to death, and that she would keep us posted. Chris was watching my face for any signs of what was going on. When I hung up, I tried to string a story together, but nothing was making sense. I tried to get more information from my mother but she was a wreck.

I held onto the phone for hours that night. Finally grandma called me back to say Uncle Jim wasn't doing well. She said to get some sleep and she would update me tomorrow. Needless to say, it was hard to sleep that night.

I got up and went to the daycare center where I was a teacher. I was trying to keep a smile on my face for the kids, but it must have been noticeable that I wasn't really all there. Eventually my boss coaxed out of me what was going on. Like the night before, I tried to string together what little I knew about what had happened- just that my uncle was badly hurt from a fall he took while walking. That's when she told me about a website called Caring Bridge that a family friend of hers used when she was undergoing chemotherapy. The website was a place where the family could keep others up-to-date on the patient. She wrote it down for me on a scrap of paper. I stuffed it in my pocket.

When I got home late that afternoon, things were still fuzzy. All I knew was Uncle Jim had made it through the night, and now most of the day. My mom and dad were at the hospital when I got home, and I was hoping they would be able to tell me more once they returned.

It turned out that I wasn't the only one who was worried and who wanted to know more about what was going on. My Aunt Mary Ann and Uncle John were getting a ton of messages on their answering machine from people desperate to find out if Jimmy was going to come out of this. That's when I remembered the website my boss had given me. I gave the address to my Aunt Mary Ann, and the next day the website for Uncle Jim was up and running. My Aunt and Uncle updated it as often as there was any news, good or bad. Word of it spread around, and people from all over the country- and world- who knew Jimmy were writing and posting messages. The guestbook on the website was what people flocked to. Many wrote that they were praying for him; others wrote about memories and happy thoughts they had about my Uncle Jimmy. By reading those entries in the guestbook, any stranger who didn't know Jimmy would be able to tell how loved he was, how many lives he had touched.

I was glad the guestbook would be there for him to read when he woke up, which I knew in my heart would happen.

- Jenesis Campbell

First Quarter of a
Four Quarter Game

Caring Bridge website- Journal:

Friday, November 20, 2009

John & I went to see Jim tonight. He's doing ok. He has a slight fever again so they keep taking blood for cultures to stay on top of that. They did put the central line in today to draw blood. They might take the breathing tube out tomorrow but it all depends on how much Jim will be able to tolerate the pain. They intubated him because his pain was too much and the morphine for the pain suppresses respiration, so he wasn't getting a good amount of air in to his lungs. John & I are still amazed at how many breaks, fractures and cracks he actually has. I told him he is on the internet and that he has his own website now.

Mary Ann Bay

Sunday, November 22, 2009

Mom & Dad went & spent time with Jim today. Aunt Barbara came up from Westchester as well. Things seem to be status quo for today. Jim slept most of the time. His vital signs & general informa-

tion are either leveled off or rising for the better. At this time (9PM) Diana and Dave Carman visited with Jim and were able to actually give him a kiss goodnight without interfering with any of the machines. There is still hope that the intubation tube will be removed in the next few days- maybe by Thanksgiving.

Mary Ann Bay

I remember once, when we were small kids, my mom got mad at my brother, John. They were in the kitchen, and after my brother sprinted into the living room I heard my mom going for the wooden spoon. My parents rarely hit us in any way, so John must have done something particularly bad. I threw my brother a hardcover book that was near me and told him to shove it down the backside of his pants. When my mother came into the room she took a swing at John's butt with that spoon. But with a loud *crack!* the spoon shattered. John and I laughed 'till we cried. My mom started laughing too. After that, she forgot all about what had made her upset. Now that I was in the hospital, John was there every day. He was the one doing most of the talking to the doctors and hospital staff, and he and his wife Mary Ann filed for New York State disability for me. He brought me socks for my cold feet and an electric toothbrush. Once upon a time I had watched his backside. Now that I was in the hospital, he was watching mine.

Caring Bridge website- Journal:

Thursday, November 26, 2009

Thanksgiving Day: *John got to the hospital at 11 AM and had to wait until 1 PM to see Jim. Jim was having tests done. Mom & dad came too. John, mom & dad were able to chat with Jim. He was able to eat applesauce. The family felt thankful for the day and it seems like we're heading in the right direction. We are thankful for all of the people that have been visiting this site and leaving messages in Jim's guestbook. We feel that all of your prayers have helped Jim to start on his road to recovery.*

Mary Ann Bay

On Thanksgiving Day, after ten days in the ICU, I was moved to a new room in the Med/Surg Unit. My breathing and feeding tubes were pulled. Unfortunately, my Thanksgiving dinner in the hospital was inedible. No fault of the hospital staff: since I still couldn't eat solid food, my turkey and stuffing and gravy were pureed into a gruel straight from *Oliver Twist*. I tried one bite- or more accurately, one sip- and gave up. I felt somewhat depressed on Thanksgiving because I couldn't be with my family at home. But I received a visit from my family and my friend Lonnie, and that cheered me up a bit.

It was around this time, after the breathing tube had been removed, when I could finally speak, that I began telling others, as best I could, what happened that night. When I said I walked to my neighbor's house, some jaws dropped. "Walked? With 23 broken bones? You mean crawled."

"No," I said, "walked."

While I was laid out on her lawn, I wanted to tell my neighbor about seeing God. I wanted to tell the paramedics, the doctors and nurses. After I awoke from my coma, I wanted to tell anyone who had ears to hear. But I knew if I started talking about seeing God that people would think me nuts, that I had left most of my brain smashed on the rocks down in the culvert. So I decided to tell one family member at a time, quietly, rather than make some sort of evangelical presentation before everyone. It was my mom who happened to be alone with me first, so I told her about the Light and about seeing God. I didn't tell her about the angel who had visited me in the hospital. After my mom, I told my sister, then my brother, and finally my dad. They questioned me: "Are you sure you weren't hallucinating from loss of blood?" In the end they believed me, or else were too polite to argue with a guy laid out in a hospital bed. But they all told me that *something* miraculous must have happened that night. How does a guy with 23 broken bones, including 10 vertebrae, climb up out of a 14 foot deep culvert and walk more than two hundred feet to his neighbor's house? And, perhaps thinking about how others might receive such a story, they told me before making a claim about seeing God that I'd better be sure. I told them I'd never been surer of anything in my life.

Hit Him and Hold Him

My brother Jimmy had been walking pretty consistently every day, rain or shine- or snow- for nearly a good solid year, in some cases getting in 5-6 miles a day, 25-30 miles a week, around 100 miles a month. We would come back from work landscaping- Jimmy and I have worked together in my business for 26 years- at 5 or 6 o'clock at night, and we would end up chatting in the truck in the parking lot for a good half hour or more, discussing all the things that happened that day- what got done, what didn't get done, what needed to get done tomorrow- along with thoughts about our family gas station or other things. Jimmy walked to keep his weight under control. I wanted to lose weight too, so Jimmy and I realized we could kill two birds with one stone- we could have walking meetings. We figured if we could walk at a good pace of 4 to 4 ½ mph and still talk, we were getting in shape and discussing business at the same time. So we got into the regular habit of holding walking meetings after work, even to the point where we enjoyed the walks and conversations so much that we would walk on our rare days off.

On the night of November 15, 2009, I called Jimmy and asked if he wanted to go for a walk, even though it was a Sunday. Jimmy told me he was tired from metal-detecting all day, and for me to go on by myself. I went for my walk, and not long after I got home I got the phone call- "Anyone there, please pick up, Jimmy's had a bad accident. Come, please come." That's how it began, and it hasn't ended yet. Maybe it never will end. I sometimes wonder what our lives would be like now if, instead of walking down Hammertown Road, Jimmy had joined me that night for our regular walk in town. Maybe tomorrow we would be hitching up the trailers and heading out to mow lawns and build rock walls and patios. But those days are gone.

I rushed to Jimmy's house. After he was loaded into the ambulance, my parents and I sped to the hospital, not far behind. The ride was mostly in silence, each of us lost in our own thoughts, our own worst fears. Once in the hospital we made some calls: Jimmy's ex-wife, Yanina, my sister Diana, my wife, Mary Ann. We gave information about Jimmy at the front desk. We waited. And waited some more. We started to get worried: judging by the amount of time it was taking, it seemed like the doctors had an awful lot to do. After several hours of waiting, we were finally let in to see Jimmy. He was on a bed in a hospital gown. He looked bad, but not as bad as he did on his neighbor's lawn, when he was covered in blood. The doctor came over and told us he needed to speak with us. "Please step out here."

My mother asked, "How is he?" My parents were walking ahead, and the doctor turned to me and mouthed, "I don't know how he's alive." Once out of the room, the doctor then spoke to all three of us. "He's bad. So far we've found a number of broken ribs, a fractured skull, he's lost a lot of blood..." and then his voice trailed off into a list of bones that completely lost us. We all wanted to know one thing. My mom asked, "You'll bandage him up and send him home, right?"

"Ma'am," the doctor said, turning to my mom, "he's not going anywhere."

"But he's going to be okay, right?"

"We don't know that. He's in very bad shape. He's hurt himself tremendously."

At 2 AM they told us the best thing to do was to go home. And so we reluctantly left Jimmy, not exactly thinking he would die, but not knowing if he would live. The ride home was even quieter than the ride to the hospital. We all realized that in an instant, our entire lives had changed. My parents were supposed to leave for Las Vegas the next day. We were due to re-open our family gas station soon, with Jimmy taking a lead role in that. Those plans were stopped in their tracks. We got home about 3 AM. I talked to my wife and together we cried ourselves to sleep.

We returned to the hospital on Monday afternoon. Jimmy was trying to talk but had trouble breathing. He held Mary Ann's hand. He was hooked up to machines. In the few hours we were there,

45

Jimmy's condition deteriorated and the doctors told us they needed to induce him into a coma. After that, it became a vigil. For the next several days our family took turns sitting with Jimmy.

On the second or third night Mary Ann and I were told we couldn't see him right away. Neither of us wanted to sit in the hospital, so we drove to Barnes and Noble, a store Jimmy and I sometimes went to together to browse, and bought some metal-detecting magazines. It was tough bringing those magazines back to the hospital to place on the table beside Jimmy's bed, because I didn't know if Jimmy would ever wake up, whether he would ever read those magazines.

Days later we were told again that Jimmy's condition was serious, and that any number of complications could occur, including pneumonia. He had had a serious allergic reaction to medication, which caused a horrible rash. We were told on the Monday before Thanksgiving that if Jimmy didn't improve soon, we would need to consider funeral arrangements. Those were not words I had ever expected to hear.

Jimmy is trusting and good-natured. He never fights with anyone, doesn't do drugs, doesn't drink, is always ready to help. I remember not long before his accident he refused to drive the truck and trailer down the road because one of the taillights was broken and he didn't want to get a ticket. I could see the place we wanted to bring the trailer- it was just down the road- and we knew every cop in town, but still Jimmy wouldn't do it. He's that kind of person. But in 26 years of landscaping, I've never had a better worker. Jimmy is tough, and a fighter. If I didn't know that already, a phone call from my cousin Rich should have convinced me: "You've got to see it, it's farther than you think, it's no roll down a hill." And then, Jimmy started to try to breathe on his own, as though he had heard what the doctors had told us. I didn't know what was going on behind his closed eyes, but I knew he was fighting. If he had anything to do with it, there weren't going to be any funeral arrangements.

By Thanksgiving Day, Jimmy's condition had improved. My folks went to see him in the morning, and I went for the second shift, for the afternoon. It was a beautiful fall day- sunny, cloudless blue sky, crisp air. I wasn't allowed to see Jimmy right away, so I sat outside for a few hours in the parking lot, making some calls. When I got to see him, Jimmy had been brought out of the coma, but he wasn't completely awake. He was propped up with pillows. He still seemed groggy, shifting in and out of consciousness. The window was open and the cool air was drifting in. I put on some football games, and as I flipped through the channels I told Jim what teams were playing. And then Jimmy did something that made it seem to me like the world had split open and some shining miracle had come streaming through: he nodded his head when he wanted me to stop at a game. For the first time in a while I thought, He might just make it. I'll never forget it: the cool air drifting in through the window, the sounds of the football games, my brother out of a coma and alive and nodding his head. It was the best damn Thanksgiving I've ever had. Despite the tragedy, we all had so much to be thankful for.

I'm Jimmy's older brother, and I've always looked out for him. When we were younger, Jimmy would pick on me about my schoolwork, because I struggled with reading and grades, and I would pick on him, like all brothers do. But one thing I rarely teased Jimmy about was his weight. But I was the only person who could; if anyone else picked on my brother, I would kick the crap out of them. One day at high school football practice a guy was picking on him- calling him fat to the point where Jimmy was in tears. So I cut into line for break-away tackles, and I ripped this guy's head off. In practice I hit Jimmy too, and hit him good. I wanted to challenge him: "Come on Jim, you can do it!" But there was always a moment in the hit when I would wrap my arms around my brother, so that I was hitting him and holding him at the same time.

In November 2009, Jimmy was hit, and hit hard. When he landed on the bottom of that ravine on those jagged rocks, it must have felt like he'd been tackled by an entire football team. I didn't know then, and still don't today, whether we will ever have walking meetings again, whether things will ever be like they used to. But I knew this much: there in the hospital, and maybe for a long time after, Jimmy would need someone to hold him. And just like at football practice, just like a million other times in our lives, through thick and thin, despite all the hits that life has thrown at us, that someone would be me.

- John Bay

In the Med/Surg Unit I had a night nurse whose name was Robert. One night we were talking about my accident and I told him I wasn't sure what had happened to my body. He couldn't believe I didn't know yet, so he went and got my chart and we went over it together. Quite suddenly, lying there in bed, I felt like Evil Knievel. The amount of damage was too much for me to take in.

I was thirsty all the time. I told Robert I loved diet ginger ale. He brought me a can to drink, and after I took a sip I said, "Ahhhhh, that's like heaven to me." After that, he would often come into my room and ask me, "Want a little bit of heaven?"

If only he'd known, I'd already seen a little bit of Heaven.

The nurse's call button became my best friend. When you're glued to a bed and can't do the simplest things by yourself, even sit upright, the call button begins to feel like an umbilical cord, your lifeline to the world. After I came out of my coma, whenever I woke up in the night I would immediately look to make sure the call button was nearby. If it was farther than arm's length, I would panic. More often than not, when I didn't see the button near, I realized I was lying on it. Often, in my sleep, it would get wrapped up in the sheets and wedged under me. After a while, the call button poking me in the back became as aggravating as a stone in my shoe. I'm a big guy as it is, and I had broken 11 ribs, so trying to get that call button out from under my body was not only painful, but comical. I would shift this way and that, trying to reach under my back. But I had broken my left shoulder blade, so that arm was out of commission. The whole process often took me half an hour. One day while I was trying to get the call button out from under me, it fell to the floor. Without that button I felt helpless. I could have started screaming, but I didn't feel ready for such drastic measures just yet. I managed to reach the wire to the call button, and when I pulled it I yanked it out of the wall. A nurse

48

came rushing into my room and asked if everything was okay. I told her what I had done, that I had pulled the call button out of the wall. She calmly said when patients did that (thank God then, I wasn't the only one) it sets off an alarm and alerts the nurses that there is a problem.

The afterglow of seeing God had not left me, but I slipped back into habitual negative thoughts to a certain degree- wondering why this had happened to me, whether I would ever get out of the hospital, feeling depressed and resentful. But in the dark of night, amid the buzz and eerie glow from the monitors, the sounds of other patients coughing or calling out for help, I realized that I had a call button to God, a direct line to Heaven. Prayer.

And so I prayed.

I received a call from Yanina and my children, Logan and Lauryn. While I was in the coma, I thought my kids had come to see me. After I woke up I asked about them, and it was then I found out they hadn't visited at all. Yanina had been telling them I'd lost my cell phone, and that's why I hadn't called much over the past few weeks. She didn't want them to see me in the hospital, and that was a decision, with hindsight, I supported. And so there in the hospital, amid the beeping machines and nurses bustling in and out and calls over the PA system, I tried my best to sound as though nothing was out of the ordinary. They asked me what I'd been up to, and I told them I'd been working hard, which wasn't exactly a lie (though I neglected to say the work I'd been doing wasn't mowing lawns and building walls but fighting for my life). No sound in the world could have been better than my kid's voices. I didn't say goodbye; that felt like the wrong thing to say. "See you soon," I told them, and I hoped with all my heart that was true.

As soon as the paramedics arrived on my neighbor's lawn, they put me in a neck brace. In addition, a back brace was measured and made for me while I was in a coma. The brace was a two piece hard shell, with front and back carapaces like a turtle. In bed I didn't need to wear the back brace, but I wasn't allowed to rise off the bed without being in it. So, once the doctors decided I should start getting out of bed a bit in the trauma unit, that brace and I became very well acquainted. I had to be rolled onto my right side- the side with an unbroken shoulder and fewer broken ribs- while the brace was slid under my back, and then rolled onto my back while the front piece was fitted over my chest. The brace was held together by Velcro straps. The first time I sat in a chair with my brace I noticed that something was wrong. I'm no doctor, but the brace seemed the wrong size for me- when sitting, the front shell came all the way up past my mouth and the sides dug into my armpits. I mentioned this to the nurses, but was told it just needed to be made tighter. But the tighter it was made, the more uncomfortable it became. Besides the ill-fit and awkward shape, that brace was hot as hell. As much as I wanted to see my kids, as much as I wanted to walk again, as much as I longed to get out of the hospital and home to my own bed, I wanted out of that brace.

Caring Bridge website- Journal:

Tuesday, December 1, 2009

Aunt Barbara visited Jim with extensive research for some possibilities of places that Jim could go to for his rehab. Jim wanted to be as close to home as possible. Later on in the afternoon there was more serious discussion by the hospital and family to get Jim out of the hospital, now that his internal vitals were stable. This would also help to prevent further infection and ultimately pneumonia. The ultimate realization is that Jim is going to need many weeks and months of intense help & rehabilitation. This hospital stay is only the first quarter of a four quarter game.

Mary Ann Bay

HOSPITAL COURSE AND TREATMENT: The patient had a significant prolonged hospital course that included intubation, mechanical ventilation, sedation on the ventilator, Neurosurgery consultation as well as Hematology and Cardiology. The patient over significant periods of time made clinical progress and after a significant period of time in the Intensive Care Unit with maximal intensive care supportive therapy, the patient eventually progressed, eventually weaned from the ventilator. The patient was fitted with a TLSO brace and intense physical and occupational therapy, acute pain management and significant supportive care. He was able to transition to the Medical/Surgical Floor where he continued to be hemodynamically and clinically stable. The patient at this point is much improved since his admission. He is clinically stable for discharge to a rehab facility.

In October 2000 our son Robert walked into the living room and showed Yanina and me his feet. His feet were swollen. He told us they didn't hurt, but seemed to be getting worse as the days went by. I thought he might have been bitten by a spider. Yanina brought him to the doctors for a check-up.

After a great number of visits and tests, the doctors told us Robert was suffering from kidney disease. One of his kidneys was not functioning at all, and the other didn't have much function. Our little son James had died not long before, and I'm ashamed to say one of my first thoughts was to curse God and wonder why, after all we had been through, this was happening to us. Robert had always been so healthy.

Robert was only 13, and he didn't show his emotions, so we could only imagine what he was thinking. But the doctors were clear with him, and so were we. He was told the score: he knew it was going to be a lot of work.

None of us knew just how much work.

Things got real crazy real quick. At this time both my wife and I were working. Robert was having blood tests done at a hospital about twenty minutes away three or four times each week. Luckily, Yanina had the graveyard shift, from 11 pm to 7 am, so she could bring Robert to his appointments. But her sleep suffered. Jon, Robert's twin brother, was scared. He thought if there was something wrong with Robert, since they were twins, there might be something wrong with him too.

It was decided that Robert needed to go to a dialysis center. The nearest was the pediatric dialysis center at the Albany Medical Cen-

ter, more than an hour from our home. At Albany Med, Robert had a biopsy done to try to determine the cause of his kidney disease. The doctor who performed the biopsy was an older doctor about to retire. He told us he was unable to perform the biopsy because Robert's kidneys were "like shoe leather". Robert, he said, was one of only five patients in all his years of practice on whom he couldn't perform a biopsy.

Now that Robert was going to Albany three or four times each week, he started missing a lot of school. Yanina had the same work schedule but now had to spend many of her days in Albany. During that time, she slept only two or three hours each day. I took Robert when I could, but I worked outdoors landscaping during the days, so it was difficult to get days off.

Very soon we came to a decision point: either hemodialysis at the hospital three or four times each week, or peritoneal dialysis at home. Because we were having so much trouble getting enough time for all the hospital visits, peritoneal seemed an option worth considering. The biggest drawback was that we would need training on the dialysis machine and everything related to it. My wife and I and Jon felt up to this. Robert felt up to this. But another obstacle was space. The supplies for the dialysis are delivered once each month and take up a lot of room, as does the dialysis machine. At the time, we were living in a small cottage we had bought in a foreclosure. When we bought it, the house was rundown with no running water, but we were excited to have a place of our own. And, let's just say the price was right. We fixed it up on the outside so it wasn't an eyesore for the neighborhood and did a little work inside. The house was only 990 square feet, and Robert's room barely had enough space for a twin bed and a dresser. We were stunned when officials from the hospital visited our home and told us our cottage was too small to support peritoneal dialysis.

Our only option was to buy a bigger house. So that's what we did. We found a house only a mile from our cottage. It was only marginally larger than our cottage, 1,200 square feet, and though none of us were in love with it we bought it because we needed to *move quickly. We couldn't sell our cottage right away and so, though we had no intention of doing so, we became landlords.*

I've never really been able to put much money away, but there always seemed like there was enough to pay bills and do a few fun things besides, like going out to dinner and the movies or taking a little weekend trip to a casino. I never had much in the way of material possessions but was always satisfied with what I had. I am of the frame of mind where you make sure the wife has the better car; I would be satisfied with a car that might have a few dents and not look so pretty but got me from point A to point B and then hopefully back again. But soon after Robert was diagnosed, I noticed that the little extra money we usually had after paying bills was gone. Then, a few months after that, I began to notice that we were having trouble even paying our ordinary bills for groceries and gas and utilities and car insurance. Yanina was working full-time for New York State, and I was working full-time as a landscaper, but even with two full-time jobs we were having trouble making ends meet. We not only had a sick child, but three other children who also needed to be provided for. Our credit card bills started to climb, not from want but from need. Many nights, before dinner was served, we would get a call from the hospital. Bring Robert now, as soon as you can. So we would turn off the stove, pile the kids into the car, and drive to the hospital. We would wait with the kids while Robert was being tested, and soon we would realize that no one had eaten. We didn't have enough cash, but we had credit cards and so that's what we used. Then to get home in the car that we'd put 40,000 miles on since Robert was diagnosed, we needed gas. We would use the credit cards again.

My wife had good health insurance through her job with the State, and that's what we were using for Robert. But all the co-pays that go along with it turned out to be like a second mortgage. Or, in our case after buying a larger home and still paying for our first, a third. Robert was on about fifteen different medications. We were being buried by the co-pays for blood work, doctors, and hospital stays, even with insurance. It got so bad that, out of desperation to *save some money, though Robert was supposed to go to a doctor for a shot a few times each week, with a nurse's permission and instruction, I decided to give him the shots myself. If we didn't have insurance, we would have gone bankrupt quickly. But even with insurance, if someone in your family is very ill, it's just a slower path to financial ruin. I know many families can relate to our experience. And in America, in the 21st century, all I can say is- what a shame.*

Now that it had been decided that Robert would undergo peritoneal dialysis, we all had to receive training on how it was done. My wife and I and Jon had to learn how to hook Robert up to the machine and how to maintain the machine so it would perform. One of the most important things was that everything needed to be sterile to prevent infections. Although we were all trained, our idea was that since Robert was a teenager, he would do most of it himself.

The big day came when the machine and supplies were delivered. We saw right away that we had made the right decision moving to a bigger house. All the boxes would have taken up the entire living room in our cottage. As it was, even in our larger house, the roof beams and walls could have used some moving.

We all felt a certain relief not having to make so many trips up to Albany. There were still lots of visits to the hospital for blood tests, but these were manageable. One of the benefits of peritoneal dialysis was that Robert was able to eat a greater variety of foods.

All in all it seemed a fairly smooth learning curve; we all got the hang of it soon enough. One night, though, the machine stopped working. Nothing was set up to be used by hand, but, improvising, that is what we did. Robert hooked up to a drain bag on the floor and emptied himself. Then I set up the fill fluid bag above him and opened the valve so the proper amount would drain into him. The fluid needed to remain in him for a certain amount of time. We had to do this entire process six times throughout the night. Luckily, my wife Yanina was still working nights, so she called us to wake us up each time we needed to do it. We made it through the night and a new machine was delivered the next morning.

Robert needed a kidney transplant. The most obvious choice would be his twin brother, Jon, but in New York State you need to be 18 to donate an organ. So Yanina, Robert's aunt, a friend of the family and I were tested. I didn't match. Yanina did, but there were other significant health concerns for her. So it was Robert's aunt who matched and volunteered to be the donor.

Robert was 15 when he had his kidney implant operation. Yanina and I waited in the surgery waiting room with a pager we'd been given sitting on the table beside us. We were worried, of course, but not only about Robert: Yanina's sister Natalie was in that operating room too, and to have two family members in there was tough to bear. But through it all I kept myself upbeat with the realization that if the operation went well, Robert would no longer need to be on dialysis. My mind would stray into the negative what ifs, but I would quickly bring my thoughts back to a positive outcome for my stepson.

The operation was a success. Though Robert needed another operation to remove his catheter, and was still taking a lot of medication and still had to have regular blood tests, he was able to return to school and continue his studies. Over the next few years, he still missed too much school for his visits to the doctor, but at least he was off dialysis and back with his classmates.

After his transplant, one of Robert's doctors at Albany Med told us that Robert would qualify for the Make-A-Wish Foundation. After we filled out the application, Robert was accepted. When it came time for Robert to make a wish, he asked his little brother Logan where he would like to go if he could. Logan said Disney World, and so that became Robert's wish.

Robert had one more wish. Two men from the Make-A-Wish Foundation were assigned to us, and Robert asked them if his Aunt Natalie, who had donated his new kidney, could come. That wish was granted, too, and Robert was thrilled. A few days before we were scheduled to fly from Albany to Orlando, the men came to the house to give us all the details of the trip and to present gifts for all the kids to bring on the plane. The day we were scheduled to leave a van arrived at our house and drove us all to the airport in Albany. When we got to our gate, we discovered that because we were a Make-A-Wish family, we were to get on the plane first. We sat up front. Before take-off the pilot came back and asked Robert if he wanted to start the plane. Robert said he wished his little brother Logan could start it. So Logan, 5 years old, went with the captain into the cockpit and started the plane.

Everything was arranged for us from the airport in Orlando. We were given a rental car and directions to Give Kids the World, an organization for kids who are sick, where we would be staying. We had a bungalow, with swimming pools and mini-golf. It was hard not to smile while there, seeing all those kids laughing and playing, but the smile was tinged with the knowledge that many of those kids wouldn't live to see their next birthdays. At Disney, we went to almost all the parks. Since Robert was a Make-A-Wish kid, we went to the front of all the lines. Make-A-Wish gave us some money, and we went to the indoor flea markets near Orlando.

When we returned to New York, Make-A-Wish asked Robert if he would be a spokesperson with some other kids and make a radio commercial to help with fundraising. After all they had done for us, it was the least we could do, and Robert agreed.

In 2004, Robert became quite sick again. His body was rejecting his transplanted kidney, and he needed again to go on dialysis. To all of us, it seemed we were back at square one. Back in the first quarter of a four quarter game.

The Guy Who Fell
Off the Road

Caring Bridge website- Guestbook:

Monday, November 23, 2009

Jimmy:

You have overcome so much in your life, I am so sorry that this has happened! I am sending prayers and positive thinking your way. I still remember in grade school when your mother brought you to school in your little radio flyer wagon when you broke your leg! Denise and I will be to visit as soon as we get the word! If there is anything that you or your parents need, I am always here for all of you.

Love,

Julie M.

In the winter of 1971/72, when I was 6 years old, I fell while ice-skating and broke my femur. To this day I can hear myself screaming when it happened. At the hospital they put a full cast on my leg from my toes up to my hip. It took a while to get used to the cast, and to the crutches, too. But after a while I was confident enough to sleep in my bedroom on the second floor, and when I came down the stairs everyone in the house knew it because I would slide down the stairs on my rear-end. I was out of school for 10 weeks and had a tutor come to my house. But midday, my mom would load me into a little red Radio Flyer wagon and pull me over to the school so I could be with my friends at recess. My friends Marc, Julie and Denise pulled me around the playground in my wagon. I couldn't imagine a better life as a 1st grader: able to hang out with friends at recess, but not having to actually go to school. As I was being carried on a stretcher into rehab, with all eyes on me, I was thinking of that 6 year-old again, riding around the playground in his Radio Flyer wagon.

Caring Bridge website- Journal:

Thursday, December 3, 2009

YEAH! A STEP FORWARD: THE BIG MOVE

As of this afternoon Jim was able to be stabilized for an ambulance drive from St. Francis Hospital to Ferncliff Rehabilitation at the Ferncliff Nursing Home located in Rhinebeck, NY. The trip wound up being rather difficult but he is settled in a private room where he will start his rehabilitation for an unknown length of time. Today was his first full real day of no oxygen, no IV. Jim is still heavily medicated for the pain. Within the next few days, as we understand it, Jim will be allowed to have visitors. Today was the first real day that the family was able to take a deep breath & breathe (Dad actually spent ½ of the day sleeping & mom came home early (5pm) so she could eat dinner and go to bed). Goodnight Jim, we all love you! From your web family.

Mary Ann Bay

My first Friday night in rehab, one of the nurse's aides was supposed to give me a sponge bath, but for some reason it never happened. When Saturday night came and no one had mentioned anything about a bath to me again, I figured it was forgotten. That night a nurse's aide came to my room. Her name, she told me, was Katrina, like the hurricane. "I tell everyone that," she said, "so they won't forget my name." She told me I was being awfully quiet, and wondered if there was anything she could do for me. I had to overcome some embarrassment, but I told Katrina I was tired of using bedpans and that it would be great if I could use the bathroom. The only problem was we needed to put on my back brace, and none of the nurses or nurse's aides had done it yet. But Katrina figured it out and helped me into it. Once inside the bathroom, though, I needed another hand. With my back brace on, I couldn't reach behind myself, so certain necessities were impossible for me to do alone. Anyone who has ever been in a similar situation will tell you it takes a lot of courage and humility to surrender all your privacy, but there really is no other choice. After she helped me, Katrina asked me if there was anything else she could do. Again it took some courage, but now that I was out of the ICU and in rehab and somewhat more awake and coherent, I wanted to start taking better care of myself. I wouldn't be dating any time soon, but a man's got to look his best. So I asked her to give me a sponge bath. It was my first sponge bath in more than a week. As far as I'm concerned, Katrina has an automatic pass into Heaven.

A nurse's aide who helped me a great deal was Pat. With hindsight, she was that perfect balance for a rehab nurse between making sure I was taken care of but also pushing me to stay focused on the goal of going home: Love you, but I'll be glad to see your backside heading out that door. I like cereal for breakfast, but some mornings there wouldn't be any cereal on my tray. I mentioned this to Pat, and five minutes later she came into my room with an armful of little cereal boxes. "A lot of people don't eat them," she said, putting the boxes into a drawer next to my bed, "but I know you will." Over the next few weeks, that cereal drawer came in handy many mornings.

The rehab building is a nursing home, and they keep it warm, so I often felt like a loaf of bread in an oven, especially in my braces. But the nurses opened the window in my private room, even though it was December, and got me a fan. My back brace had become so uncomfortable that my family was willing to pool their money to buy me a new one, since we were told insurance probably would not. One day the technician who manages all the prostheses and braces for the rehab unit saw me in my brace, head retracted in it like a turtle in its shell. He forcefully told my Physical Therapist, Mike, "No way you can leave that guy in that brace a minute longer!" The technician and Mike went to the higher-ups and got permission to cut it down. "Good news," Mike told me, not too many days before Christmas. "We're going to cut it." That technician didn't have a white beard, he wasn't particularly jolly, but he was like Santa Claus to me all the same.

When I woke up from the coma and could understand things a bit better, everyone in my family told me about the Caring Bridge website that had been set up for me. Throughout those days in the hospital, though I hadn't read any of the comments yet, my brother or mother or sister would come into my room and say, "You're up to 27 messages." Next day, my father would say, "You're up to 32 messages." By January, when I finally went home, there were more than one hundred, from friends and family from around the country and the world.

It was my sister-in-law Mary Ann who first read me one of the comments left in the guestbook. She and John wheeled me into the room at the rehab center where there were a few computers for patients to use. She pulled up the site and read me the message posted by my neighbor Indira:

Monday, November 30, 2009
Jim,
My thoughts and prayers are with you for a speedy recovery. I am so glad you saw the lights on at my house and used every ounce of strength you had in you to make it to my front door to ask for help. Although you had so much blood running down your face, I recognized you. Considering the pain you were in, as you were collapsed on my front lawn, you were still able to give me the phone number for your brother, tell me what happened to you while walking, and tell me where your pain was while I was on the phone with 911. I was in such a panic. The 911 operator asked me to wrap a towel around

your head. I was in shock when I saw the terrible gashes in your head. I cannot imagine how much pain you were in. God must have helped you make it to my front door. Good luck and get well soon!

Your neighbor, Indira

Mary Ann then showed me how many messages were on the site. I was overwhelmed. On the webpage, too, were pictures of where I fell. Until that time, I had no idea where I had fallen. It was dark when I fell, and I didn't often walk that way down Hammertown Road. I simply had no recollection of where I had tumbled down into the gully. Seeing those pictures was quite emotional for me. I wasn't sure I ever wanted to visit that place on Hammertown Road again, not even virtually or in pixels, not even in memory. But there was one thing I noticed when I looked at those pictures: there, along the side of the road, was the log I had held onto for dear life after I climbed up out of the ditch, the log I was clutching when I saw God. Seeing the log in the pictures just as I had described it to my family, just as I remembered it, was confirmation for me that I was not insane.

A few days later I wheeled myself over to the computer and logged on by myself. I wasn't able to read all the messages, partly because there were so many, but more than that because the messages brought tears to my eyes. It amazed me then, and still does to this day, how many people had written, how many people cared.

Caring Bridge- Guestbook:

Saturday, November 21, 2009

Hi Uncle Jimmy,

We miss you and we wish we could see you but we are not old enough. We keep you in our hearts. We send lots and lots and lots of love.

Love,

Holly, Heather and Joshua

Sunday, November 22, 2009

I wasn't sure what to say on here so I guess I'll just say this. Of all the people I've ever met on this journey of life there's only one person I know that could have sustained a fall like that and got up to find help. That one person is Jimbo.

There's no doubt in my mind that making it across that road will be the hardest part of your recovery my friend. I shall see you soon and I know that you will be back with us soon to hunt for treasure, tell us stories, eat pretzel and cheese sandwiches and of course make fun of the Yankees.

Eric D.

Monday, November 23, 2009
Jim,

I was shocked to hear about your accident. I have had you and your family in my thoughts and prayers. Even though it's been 26 years (yikes!) since we graduated high school together, we all share a unique bond and our classmates are special to us. We may lose touch in the day to day, month to month, year to year, but we never forget the people we shared those impressionable years with, and you have never left my memories. And now you have moved to the front of my thoughts and I send positive vibrations your way. We don't know why bad things happen to good people, but we know there is always a higher good. Bless you Jimmy. I love you. Get well soon!

Haakon O.

Monday, November 30, 2009
Hello My Friend!!

Bubba you need to gather all of your inner strength and get well!! I know we haven't kept up like we should, not many days go by that I don't tell my friends down here in Virginia a Bubba Bay story... Even though it's been since our 20th reunion when I last talked to you, I still know you're the man!! and I still have a great big place in my heart for you!!!! Get Well My Friend, GET WELL!!!!!!

With All MY Love and Prayers!!...Rick "Sugar Bear" H.

With letters like those, full of enthusiasm, not to mention lots of exclamation marks, I couldn't help but feel better. All the thoughts and prayers being directed my way helped, too. But one thing I figured out very soon after arriving at rehab was that, despite all the support, if you want to get out of there and go home, it's up to you. Rehab is tough. All the people there- the therapists and doctors and nurses- are there to help, but regaining strength and doing the exercises is your responsibility. Like almost everything in life, you get out of it what you put into it.

Every day I received occupational therapy, which for me was mostly learning how to dress myself and take care of personal hygiene. After OT with Kristin it was off to PT, where I would do leg lifts, knee raises, and toe raises in my wheelchair. Over the weeks, I progressed to standing up and sitting down in my wheelchair, and then eventually to walking with a walker. While out of my chair I would do knee bends, then some light stairs.

Before I was taken to rehab, I was told by the hospital staff that the key to recovery is getting out of bed and staying out of bed as much as I could. I never let that advice out of mind, and when I got to rehab I set a goal: get out of bed in the morning and stay out until 5 PM. I was required to wear my braces out of bed. Encased in my braces, I felt like a knight dressed in battle armor. And what a battle it was. I had trouble doing the simplest things we all take for granted. Even holding a pen in my hand and moving my fingers and wrist to sign the checks for December's bills my mom brought in (those bills were due, whether I was in the hospital or dead), sent bursts of pain through my ribs, my upper back, my neck and shoulder.

At times I became depressed. Many a night at rehab I cried myself to sleep. I sunk into times of despair, of self-pity, asking why every single thing in life needed to be so difficult, so utterly full of pain. I don't blame myself for any of it. It's only natural to feel like that. The only way I would have blamed myself was if I had sunken so deep that I couldn't get out, if I didn't remember God's gift to me. When I was at my darkest moments in the hospital and rehab, I would remember the Light.

Every day I was wheeled down to the physical therapy room. I sat next to another man a few times, and we got to chatting. "Why don't they just leave me alone to die?" he asked me one day. "My wife has been dead many years. I'm up in age and I've done what I wanted to do in life. They should just leave me alone to die." I wasn't sure what to say. For one thing, I did understand where he was coming from. And far be it for me to give advice, especially to a man who has lived twice as long as I have. But after my experience on Hammertown Road, I knew one thing: God has a purpose and a plan for all of us. So I told him I thought there is always a better reason to live than to die. I also told him that everyone who knows him wanted him to live. We were both in PT to learn to walk again unaided. But I came to see that we were there, too, to aid each other. I could bless him with my desire to live, and he could bless me with his stories and wisdom. And so each day there we sat- two men on opposite ends of things: he'd had enough and wanted out; I was grateful to be alive. Simply sitting in rehab talking to an old man I felt a gift to me from God.

I started coaching high school sports in my early-twenties. I started as an assistant winter track coach, then Junior High and Junior Varsity girls' basketball, and then for seven seasons I was the JV boys' basketball coach. All my teams came to feel like family, but my Junior High girls' team, especially, looked out for me. I'm not the world's snappiest dresser, and if I showed up to a game looking a little rumpled or wearing clothes that didn't match, my girls would refuse to be in public with me looking like that. They would ask me to change my pants, or shoes, or tie. They would tell me I had food on my jacket. If we were traveling, we would hop on the school bus and, before hitting the highway, we would swing by my house for a change of clothes.

Some people measure success by how much money they make, or whether they're promoted at work, or how many games they win. But for me, during those weeks in rehab, success was helping the therapists and nurses put on my pants and shirt. I couldn't dress myself- I couldn't even get out of bed to get my clothes. My Junior High girls would have been horrified with my wrinkled wardrobe. But I found that the more you help yourself, the easier it is for others to help you.

As a coach, I was used to pushing my players. But now the shoe was on the other foot, and they were pushing me.

Caring Bridge website- Guestbook:

Thursday, December 17, 2009

Coach 'Bubba'- I'm praying for you!!! I know you show that exceptional strength and moral courage to get better each passing day- you're a true inspiration my friend.

Best Wishes, Kevin Z.

Pine Plains Bomber for life

Thursday, December 17, 2009

Coach, I have just heard the terrible news of your accident and really don't have any idea what to say or write. You are always in my heart for what you taught me in school. I know that it was such a long time ago, but I remember like it was yesterday. I never got a chance to thank you for all that you taught all of us kids. One thing you always told us is to never give up, and always try harder. We went 35-1 with you as a JV team, and I know we would never have done that without you there. You are always with all of us even if we are miles apart. Never give up coach!

Josh "Ice" M.

***

I gave myself the nickname Bubba. When I was playing Junior High football, we were due to have a scrimmage against another team. We were given practice jerseys with no names or numbers on them. In the locker room, my teammates started writing nicknames on the backs of their jerseys. I didn't have a nickname. So I thought for a while, and Bubba came to mind. I liked the sound of Bubba Bay- all those b's and a's- and so that's what I wrote on my jersey.

And I guess the name was appropriate. When you think of 'Bubba', chances are good you think of an overweight guy. I grew up always being the fat kid. I was teased often in elementary school, and got in more than one fight because of it. I heard a lot of fat jokes.

When I was in little league, I was too fat to wear the normal-sized uniform all my friends wore. So I had to throw together a make-shift uniform. One of my coaches brought me a pair of men's softball league pants to wear. My mom made me a shirt and ironed on the letters and numbers. I was embarrassed to wear it, but I wanted to be with my friends.

When I played JV football, I couldn't fit into any of the pants. But my friends and I developed a little ritual; before the game I would slide into the legs of the extra-large jersey pants I had been given, and then three friends would grab the sides of the pants and try to lift me up and down. They would literally shake me into my pants. Once I was inside those pants, they quickly stretched out enough for me to feel comfortable to play in them.

On Varsity, I was even bigger. My team, the Pine Plains Bombers, was playing against Houstatonic on a Saturday afternoon. In pre-game warm-ups my pants split right up the back, so after I finished warm-ups I went to the sidelines and wore a rain cape so no one in the bleachers could see my split pants. When I was called in to play nose guard in the 4th quarter, I got down in my stance. As the quarterback was calling out the signals, I heard, "Holy smokes, this kid is mooning me!" One of the referees. We all started laughing, both teams, the refs, probably even people in the bleachers, and we had to hold up the game.

I played basketball at all three levels- Junior High, Junior Varsity and Varsity. Even though I was very overweight, I played often at the two lower levels. But I was a bench-warmer on varsity and hardly played at all. It bothered me, but I realized that everyone on a team has a job to do, even the fat guy. My job was to remain upbeat and be the team clown, especially at practice. When we were having a bad day at practice and the guys were tired or pissed, I would do my Meadowlark Lemon Harlem Globetrotter routine- down on the floor, turning around on my butt, dribbling the ball. It would always lighten the mood. I think Coach realized that it was an important

66

part of practice now and then, as long as I didn't try to dribble like that in a game.

In a way, I became comfortable with my weight in those years. Like a puzzle piece, I fit into my class because I was Bubba. But at that age I was becoming attracted to girls, and all the girls I wanted to date wanted to be "just friends".

The nickname Bubba stuck with me. When I got to college the name Bubba followed me there, because I wore all my sports jackets around campus. On graduation day, when my name was called out-James Michael Bay- a number of my friends didn't know it was me. They had thought all along that Bubba was my birth name.

First semester freshman year at college I weighed nearly 300 pounds. It was a tough semester for me, being away from home for the first time and missing my family and friends. I was thinking about how to survive in college, and had no time to think about losing weight. But after Christmas that year, when I returned to school, after I felt more comfortable in a college environment, I decided it was time to do something about my weight.

I went to college in Utica, New York. Winters there are cold and snowy, so I knew there would be no exercising outdoors. By second term I had left the dorms and had an apartment with some friends. I decided to exercise in my apartment. I didn't have a treadmill so I ran in place in my doorway, because this was the sturdiest part of the floor and I shook the apartment the least in this spot. I started slow and worked my way up to one hour each day of running in place. I put the radio on and ran. And ran.

I also focused more on my diet, and ate more fish and less fatty foods and snacks. My goal was to burn one more calorie than I took in for the day. Hopefully, more than one, but one would do on a bad day. I didn't put myself on a diet. I watched what I ate and if I wanted something unhealthy- if I was out with friends, say, and we were having French fries and beer- I had it. That would mean more running and less eating the next day or two.

There came a moment when I knew I could do it. It was one of those turning points in life you never forget. I had gone home with one of my roommates for some home cooking. I had one helping of the meal. His mom then brought out dessert: a great shimmering bowl of chocolate pudding with a mountain of whipped cream. I knew if I had dessert I would have to run extra time and struggle to lose what I was about to gain, so for the first time in my life I politely declined. That might seem like a small thing to most, but for a guy who has not only been very overweight his whole life but also has a serious sweet tooth, that was an accomplishment on the order of climbing Mt. Everest.

When I went home for the summer holiday, people didn't recognize me. In the five months of the semester I had lost over 80 pounds (and eventually, after the summer holiday, 115 pounds total). When my mom saw me she thought I looked unhealthy, so she set up a doctor's appointment for me. The diagnosis: healthy as a horse. I remember standing next to a friend of my mom's and she had no idea who I was until I said something. Some of the girls I had wanted to date in high school now wanted to date me. My body had changed, but I was still the same Bubba. So I politely told those girls where to go.

My first semester at college a hypnotist came to campus. Out of curiosity, I went to watch. Next thing I knew, I was onstage with a group of fellow students. I was hypnotized, and was told later I was singing rock and roll nursery rhymes- belting out Jack & Jill and Humpty Dumpty. I was over 280 pounds at that time, and was told later I was dancing around on stage, reaching into the crowd and posing like a star. Then I took off my shirt. Despite not being able to sing a lick and the sight of my belly bouncing around, I guess it went over well because quite a few people approached me on campus after that and I made a number of new friends. The next year, after I had lost all that weight, I returned to the hypnotist's show. This time I sat in the rear where I wouldn't be called onto stage. Toward the end of the show, I overheard two guys in front of me talking.

"Not a bad show."

"No, but you should have seen this show last year."

"What happened?"

"This fat guy was onstage singing rock and roll nursery rhymes. It was hysterical."

I was sitting right behind them, but they would never have recognized me.

Like most people who struggle with weight, I've been riding the roller coaster. I kept the weight off for many years, but it slowly crept back on me. When I turned 29 I was up to 235 pounds again. And so again I decided to lose weight. I got up to running six miles a day and lost 65 pounds. But once again, after I got married and got comfortable, I gained it back. After my boys died, mostly from lethargy and depression, I ballooned to 320 pounds. I lost the weight again, this time through a regimen of walking, and lost 70 pounds. I was feeling pretty good, and was walking again regularly, when I fell off the road.

At rehab I acquired a new nickname. When I first arrived I told the staff I had fallen off a road. "How do you fall off a road?" one of them asked me. Word went around the unit fairly quickly. Officially, the staff at the rehab center knew me as James Bay. Unofficially, I was The Guy Who Fell Off the Road.

A Little Bit
of Heaven

Caring Bridge website- Journal:

Wednesday, December 9, 2009

Jim hit a milestone today- he was able to take his first shower since the accident (he sat in a chair in the shower, but we're sure that it probably felt great). Another more important milestone is that Jim walked 150 feet with the help of his walker. There are still problems with being fitted with his brace. Not having the proper fit with his brace puts Jim in pain and ultimately he has not been able to do his physical therapy for as long as he needs to and to the extent that he needs to. Over the last couple of days he has been able to keep down solid food.

Mary Ann Bay

I hadn't had a real shower or washed my hair in nearly a month. I mentioned this to Steven, one of my occupational therapists. The biggest problem was that I couldn't take off my neck brace, and the brace was full of foam padding that couldn't get wet. Steven told me he had worked in another rehab unit that specialized in people with back and neck injuries, and he told me he would help me take a shower. When he came back the next day I was as excited as a boy on Christmas morning. He helped me strip down to my underwear and shorts. Then Steven put on my back brace without a shirt. He placed plastic bags around my neck brace to protect it from water, then wheeled me into the shower where I sat in a shower chair.

The following week, Steven said something I didn't expect to hear: "It's time to wash your hair." He carefully removed my neck brace and told me sternly that I wasn't allowed to move an inch. I wanted out of that neck brace so bad that I wasn't about to even bat an eyelash. Steven removed the foam and replaced it with washcloths. He put my neck brace back on and we were off to the shower room again. When you're in such a sorry state, you become grateful for the little things. Hot water streaming over my scalp (careful to avoid the spot my head was fractured), the caress of the water, the warmth seeping in through my skull and spreading down my neck, the water running down my chest and back and legs: a little bit of Heaven. Most of us, most of the time, don't notice these little miracles, these simple pleasures, but they wash over us like that water all day, every day.

Around this time I had an appointment with my back and neck doctor in Poughkeepsie. It was going to cost me a co-pay with my insurance if I took an ambulette to get there. So my dad and sister decided they would take me instead. Before I was allowed to go with them, they were trained by my PT Mike on how to help me and spot for me when I was walking. At this time I was using a walker. I rode in the front seat and, though I was very dizzy the entire trip there and back, it was as though I was seeing things through the eyes of a child. I felt wide-eyed and excited. No matter that I fell down a gully and shattered 23 bones, no matter that I'd spent the last month in the hospital and rehab: the world was still here, waiting to show me it's little miracles- a cat cleaning itself on a porch, someone walking out of Dunkin' Donuts with a steaming cup of coffee, a leaf tumbling across the road.

***

One afternoon my brother John and his wife Mary Ann handed me a manila folder filled with handwritten letters. My niece Holly had told her 4th Grade class what had happened to me, and the class decided to write to me.

Dear Uncle Jimmy,

I told my class what happened to you. My teacher Mrs. LaRobardier thought we could write letters to you. So here they are. Hope you get better soon!

Love,
Your Niece Holly

Dear Mr. Bay,

Hi my name is Martha! I heard what happened and I just wanted to say that I feel really bad when Holly told me I almost started to cry! Again I am so so sorry. We thought our letters would turn that frown upside down! So keep up your strength so you can stay healthy and happy for winter. I hope you feel better soon!

Sincerely,
Martha G.

Dear Mr. Bay

My name is Elizabeth. I'm one of Holly friends. I hope you will get out of the hospital. I hope you get out soon. Holly talked to me what happened I feel sad for you. I do it with my heart. I want to help Holly getting you out of the hospital. I hope you feel better Mr. Bay.

Sincerely,
Elizabeth R.

Dear Mr. Bay,

Hi my name is Karen and I hope you get better. Holly told me what happened and I was shocked then on Monday I heard more

from my mom. I heard you had a bad day Sunday. I heard you had
a lot of bones broken in your body. It seems ruff and you really need
some care. Your family is probably going to give care. I hope you get
better. Have a nice rest of the year.
   Sincerely,
   Karen N.

Things had definitely been 'ruff', but reading those dozen or so letters, my frown turned upside down. Kids never cease to amaze me. If we could think like kids more often, this world might just be a better place.

And speaking of upside down frowns. My room at rehab was on the second floor, down the end of the hallway. The way out to the elevators was down the hall and past the nurse's station. Another patient, Gayle, would sit in her wheelchair on the corner near the nurse's station. I would pass by her on my way to therapy sessions. No matter she was in a wheelchair in a rehab center at Christmastime, she never failed to have a smile for me. She told me I reminded her of someone in her family who had also been in a bad accident and had to wear a body brace. We got to talking, and quickly became hallway friends. She would say something encouraging to me every day. "You're looking better today than yesterday." There were dark days when I didn't feel I could do what the PTs and OTs wanted me to do, or when I felt depressed, but Gayle's smile never failed to lift my spirits.

After I was released from rehab I went back several months later to say hi to everyone. When I walked down the hall to the nurse's station, Gayle was sitting in her usual place. My braces were off, and I was walking with a cane. Gayle didn't recognize me at first without my braces, but when she did her smile lit up.

"You look better today than the last time I saw you," she said.

"You always say that."

"In your case, it's true. You do look better."

74

"Now it's your turn. Keep plugging along and you'll get out of here."

Maybe she thought she wasn't going anywhere, because a look of resignation settled on her face. But then, as she always did, she smiled.

My family- my brother and parents and often my sister- came to see me every day. I remembered all too well being in their shoes, heading off every day to the hospital to visit a loved one.

I visited my little baby son James Ulysses every day and every night in the ICU. He would have good days and bad days, but you always keep your hope up. My wife Yanina was released from the hospital after a few days, so she came with me to see our son for the first time. No matter what I said to my wife, she thought it was her fault that our little baby was in the hospital like this. I realized it would be difficult to change her mind, but I told her we cannot know why this happened. It happened, and it is in God's hands.

It's a good thing there were no rules against singing in the hospital, or they would have had to boot me out. Every day I would sing a song to my son. It was a tune I made up the second day I went to see him. When I settled down next to my son, I started singing that song, and I kept singing softly for two hours. While I sang, little James' numbers started to rise.

I went to see him on a Friday night, which was his ninth day in the hospital. The nurses were very concerned, and wanted me to know before I saw him that he was having a very bad time: his oxygen saturation numbers were down, along with lots of other numbers I didn't particularly understand. The nurses told me my voice might give him some comfort.

I sang to my little boy, and for the next hour he seemed to be doing okay. But then things started to go downhill. The doctor was called and came around 2 AM. After he had examined James, the doctor told me that he didn't think my son would make it. I broke down, and was so disconsolate that the nurses set up a chair for me to sleep in. It was a rough sleep, but I think I managed to sleep a little.

75

When I woke Saturday morning, I went to check on my son. His numbers were decent, but not great. I drove home to see my family and along the way listened to a sports recap on the radio about Friday night's game between the Mets and the Yankees. I'm a big Mets fan, and it did help a bit to listen, but no matter how many runs the Mets scored, no matter how many Yankees the Mets bullpen struck out, I couldn't get my thoughts off my little son.

My wife and I and our children decided to visit my parents. While there, we received the call.

The hospital wanted us to come down and give them permission to pull the plug so James could die peacefully. Needless to say, until my ride to the hospital after my fall into the gully, that was the longest ride I've ever made.

When we arrived at the hospital the nurses told us we could hold our son. This was the first time any of us had held little James. So the nurses wrapped him up good and tight in blankets, and each one of us got to hold him and say goodbye. My mom, dad, sister-in-law and brother were there to hold him. Jerry Stuetzle, a deacon in the Catholic church, who was my good friend Rick's father, was there to say some prayers and console us.

They asked us if we would like to hold our son after they pulled the plug until he died. Yanina and I decided we couldn't. I wanted to remember my son with his little arms and legs kicking, just as I had always seen him. And so my brother John held my son until little James died. I don't know if I've ever thanked my brother for doing that; if not, I'm doing so now. It was comforting to know our son had died in warm, loving arms.

Our son, James Ulysses Bay, died on June 10, 2000.

When my wife and I left the hospital, we thanked the hospital staff for helping our son. To the doctor who came to help deliver our son, my wife said thank you so much for taking care of our son, and no offense, but I hope I never see you again.

We didn't know whether to have a funeral service for James, but in the end decided we should, since no one had ever seen him; only family had been allowed into the hospital. Deacon Stuetzle held a service in the funeral home. The Deacon said a great many kind words, and many people attended, but since no one knew little James, the service, we realized, was mostly for us. I wrote something to read to everyone that day:

Our Little Boy

On May 30*th* at 2:54 AM our little boy James Ulysses Bay was born. He was eleven and a half inches long and weighed one pound four ounces. His gestational period was twenty-three weeks and three days. He was born at Northern Dutchess Hospital and he took his first ambulance ride to Vassar Brothers Hospital. He was admitted to the neonatal intensive care unit and his spot in the room was 1-9. Our baby was born with hands that had long fingers that he got from his mother. He also had the Bay nose and big feet like his dad. His first nurse was a wonderful lady named Thelma and God arranged her to be his last nurse. I'm reading this letter so that everyone can know that even though the doctors think he was sick from the beginning, he had seven great days. He was very active, his hands and feet were moving all over the place to the point he would knock off a wire and set alarms off. As they say, he was full of spunk and vinegar. Then the bacteria took effect and he went downhill from there, even though he was a fighter to the end. They removed the ventilator at 7:24 PM on June 10 and he died two minutes later at 7:26 PM in my brother's arms. Even though he was only here for a short time, he was our special boy who was in such a rush to see the big world. My wife, boys and I thank everyone for the support you have given us.

After the service at the funeral home, we drove to the cemetery in Elizaville and buried him there. Days after the funeral we were told by the cemetery officials that, not to wish you bad luck, but if in the future someone bigger were to die, he or she could be buried with baby James, since our son was so small. After the funeral, Yanina would not go to the cemetery at all; it was too painful for her. I did visit the cemetery, though it was very hard to do, but I felt that one of *us should go. Our little baby did not have a gravestone for five years. Yanina was so distraught that she could not help pick one out. Of course all along we both knew we would need to get a tombstone, but I was not going to make such an important decision on my own. The selection of a headstone for baby James would wait until Yanina was ready. I understood and supported my wife.*

When our son Robert died of kidney failure in 2006, we buried him with little James. So now we had two sons buried together and we needed to get a stone for the two of them. A few days after Robert's funeral we went to pick one out. I suppose, with hindsight, that it turned out for the best. We got them a nice black stone. On it are their names, dates of birth, and dates of death. We did not put any sayings or Biblical passages or any other writing on the stone. Above their names is a heart with two clasping hands. When we saw that design for the first time, in a book of designs to choose from, it seemed perfect, our two boys holding hands walking on to the Lord. And when I saw the stone in the cemetery for the first time, I realized why we had waited. Someday, maybe, there will be more hands added to that tombstone- mine and Yanina's and our other kids. But that will wait until God's time.

Caring Bridge website- Journal:

Thursday, December 10, 2009

Mom, dad & Aunt Barbara visited with Jim today. John visited as well. While John was visiting with Jim, they discussed yesterday's snowstorm and Jim was sad because other than leaving to live in Arizona this was the first storm that Jim has not plowed with John in 24 years.

There will be a family meeting with the facility next week as to when Jim can have visitors other than immediate family.

I have been a landscaper most of my adult life, working with my brother John, and as part of our business we plow snow in the winter. It saddened me when I woke up in rehab and saw the ground covered with snow, knowing I wouldn't be able to help my brother plow. I have plowed snow every winter since I was 19 years old and never missed a single storm except for the year I moved to Arizona. Even sadder was the realization that this was probably going to be a feeling I was going to need to get used to. There might be many things I was used to doing that I wouldn't be able to do in the future.

That day my brother came to visit me. John asked me if I wanted to go outside. He helped me into my coat and hat and gloves. But it was so hot in rehab that I was wearing only shorts, so he found a large towel and laid it over my lap. My brother pushed me around the parking lot in the snow in my wheelchair. He played Christmas music on his phone while he pushed me around. By then the snow was coming down pretty hard. I woke up feeling pretty depressed, but that day ended up being Christmas come early for me. And as I always did when it snowed, I thought again of baby James.

In the winter of 2000/01 we had a heavy snow, and I was out plowing a driveway in Clinton Corners. This driveway was notorious for swallowing trucks; it wasn't a long drive, but it had a slight sideways pitch to it, so that whenever anyone tried to back blade the snow in front of the garage the back end of the truck would slide towards a tree. On this night, I had already put in a very long day, and as I was pulling snow back from in front of the garage I got stuck. I got out of the truck and started to shovel the truck out. I shoveled some snow, got back in the truck and tried to move, but still the truck wouldn't budge. So I got out and started shoveling some more. After an hour I was finally able to get myself out and finish plowing.

I still had one more driveway to plow in the town of Milan. I was exhausted, but set off. Soon I came upon a truck that was off the road and stuck in a snow bank. The man asked if I could pull him out. I was dog-tired, and still had another driveway to plow. The last thing I wanted to do was spend more time out in the snow. I couldn't wait to get home. But knowing what I had just been through the last hour, I knew I had to pull him out. He was stuck pretty good, but I managed to get him out. He thanked me, and I set off to do my last driveway.

This last driveway I always thought of as being up in God's Country, because the driveway led up to a house on a hilltop. When I arrived the storm stopped and the moon came out. Unlike my last driveway, this one is long, and it took me quite a while to plow up to the house. I was tired, but with the moonlight on the snow, I thought there could be worse places in the world to be. But then I got stuck again.

I got out, shoveled, got back in and tried to break the truck free. But it wouldn't budge. I got back out of the truck, fell to my knees, and prayed that my little son James, who had passed away six months before, would come and give his father a little help. When I finished my prayer, all the lights on the truck started flashing: the headlights, the clearance lights and the blinkers, all flashed for about 10 seconds. I wasn't sure I saw what I saw, but I got back in the truck and tried to back out without shoveling. I put the truck in reverse and the truck backed out like there was no snow at all. It took me a while, sitting there in the truck, tears rolling down my cheeks, to get myself together enough to finish the plowing job.

The truck lights never blinked or flickered at all the rest of that night, and I drove that truck for many years after without a single problem with any of the lights other than an occasional blown bulb.

Little baby James: my snow angel.

III

You Lifted Up
My Soul

I'll Be Home for Christmas

The tragedies we had endured over the years wore on us, and eventually my wife Yanina and I separated about a year and a half before my fall. My children, Logan and Lauryn, who were now living in Maine with Yanina, were supposed to come visit me after Christmas, but I didn't want them seeing me in rehab. So I asked the doctors and therapists if I could go home. After some discussion, it was decided that, with lots of help, I could manage it.

Patient: James Bay
Unit: 2B
Discharge Date: December 23, 2009

James was admitted to Archcare at Ferncliff Nursing Home on December 2, 2009 from St. Francis Hospital for short term rehabilitation following a fall off an embankment at home.
James participated in a restorative physical therapy program. He currently ambulates 1000 feet with a rolling walker and close

supervision times one. He transfers independently but requires close supervision times one for car transfers. He is able to ascend/descend 24 steps without a handrail and close supervision times one. His family has been educated on how to guard during gait, stairs and car transfers. A rolling walker and hospital bed were ordered for home use. An in-home physical therapy assessment and exercise program in recommended.

James participated in an occupational therapy program and is prepared to transition home at close supervision to independent level for ADL's having assistance from family members. Use of a shower chair and grab bars is recommended for bathing. His family is able to assist with his back brace. No occupational follow-up is necessary.

Close supervision times one. At least for a time, I would need at least one person to assist me with basic tasks. That person would be my dad. He volunteered to stay with me in New York while my mom headed back to Las Vegas, where my parents live part of the year. My sister Diana, my brother John and his wife Mary Ann, along with some friends, would also be near if I needed help. I could tell my dad was a little nervous about the whole thing, and so was I. It would be up to the two of us to put my back brace on and take it off every day. It would be up to the two of us to maintain a regimen of rehab exercises. It would be up to the two of us, together 24-7, not to kill each other.

I was discharged on December 23rd. I hadn't seen my home in 38 days. The next night, Christmas Eve, my dad and I went to the Methodist Church in town. I'd been going to this church since I was a kid. I'd lapsed over the years, but had gone now and again on special occasions. If there was ever a special occasion, this was it: I was home, I was alive, and it was Christmas.

On another Christmas Eve, many years ago when I was a kid, it had snowed so much that we thought the Christmas Eve midnight service might be cancelled. I remember our family- my mom and dad and the three kids- piling into my Mom's car and driving to church. We were early, and there was no one at the church yet. So we rolled down the car windows and drove around town singing Christmas carols.

But on this night, so many years later, my dad and I kept the car windows rolled up and spared the neighborhood by not singing. The church was full. Many people had heard about my accident, and they came up to me and told me how nice it was to see me. If they only knew how nice it was to see them. Strike me with a lightning bolt, but for me, church has always been more about fellowship than about God.

As we sang Christmas carols that night, my mind kept going to one of my favorite hymns, "Here I am Lord."

> *Here am I, Lord. Is it I, Lord?*
> *I have heard you calling in the night.*
> *I will go, Lord, if you lead me.*
> *I will hold your people in my heart.*

I couldn't help but think, as I sat there in my brace in the pews, my body wracked by pain in a hundred places, despite it all: Yes, here I am, Lord, here I am.

Caring Bridge webpage- Guestbook:

Sunday, January 3, 2010

Jimmy,

So glad you're home. I'm sure your family is taking very good care of you. Keep up the PT. I know it's hard, but you can do it. Whenever I'm feeling a little down about my situation with my son, who has Cerebral Palsy, I have to remember that there is a reason for everything, even if we never discover the true meaning of that reason. You're a good person, with a strong will, and I know you will come out of this even stronger than before. We are all very close by if there is anything one of your classmates or other friends can do. Just call out to us.

Love you Bubba,

Lizzy W.

A reason for everything. As I sat in church on Christmas Eve, I thought about all I had been through over the past month and a half, over the past many years, and I wondered what the reason for it all could possibly be. Why would two sons be dead and buried? Why would I have shattered my bones and nearly died? Why had Yanina and I struggled so, and divorced? What good could possibly come of it?

When I prayed the Prayer of Jabez, I had asked God to give me something. I wondered if God had indeed answered me. What had God done for me but throw one tragedy after another my way? But sitting in the pews with the Christmas hymns echoing through the church, with Jesus who had suffered far more than me looking down on me from the Cross, I remembered the Light. God had told me that I was to do work for Him. I didn't know what I was meant to do for God. I doubted that I was worthy to do God's work. Me? Bubba Bay? But God had kept me alive. Here I was, sitting in church, when so easily I could be dead. When I first started saying the Prayer of Jabez, I could never have imagined the roads it would lead me down. I never thought I would shatter 23 bones. I never thought I would see God. I never thought I would have the courage to tell anyone about what I saw and experienced. But every time I told someone, they said, "Keep telling the story." And so as I sat in church, I decided there would be at least one thing I would try to do for God. I would tell the story of that night, about how God came to me in my time of need.

My primary motivation for getting out of rehab early was so my kids Logan and Lauryn could visit me at Christmastime at home, and not have to see me in rehab. Yanina hadn't told them about my accident. Instead, she told them my cell phone was broken and that's why I hadn't called. She thought since the kids were so far away that they would worry too much until they came to see me. But Yanina had car trouble, so they weren't able to make the long trip from Maine to New York at Christmas.

Instead of my kids, on Christmas Day I received a visit from a home health aide from St. Francis Hospital Home Health Care. At first I thought it strange she would come on Christmas, but she explained to me that the law requires her to contact me and get me set up within a certain number of days of release. She explained that, along with my dad, three other people would be helping me transition back home from the hospital and rehab: Sharon, a nurse who my insurance would allow to come four times; Nicole, an OT who would come only once; and Barbara, my PT, who would see me eight times in total. All the therapists battled the insurance company on my behalf, but none of them could get any additional visits approved. Soon after, because I had been on Yanina's New York State insurance plan and Yanina had left her job when she moved to Maine, I lost my insurance altogether. And so I was left to do most of my recovery at home, without therapists.

When I was growing up, my dad ran a gas station and mechanic shop, so he wasn't home much except Sundays when he was off. I didn't see him as much as I would have liked. That all changed after my accident. He helped me dress in the morning and put on my back brace. He did all the housework. He shoveled the snow. He took me to all my doctor's appointments. He made lunch and dinner. He helped me shower. He helped me into bed at night. My dad was 71 years old at that time. Maybe he would rather have been playing golf or pulling a few slots at a casino, enjoying his retirement. He had earned it. But now my dad was working harder than ever. He would come into my room in the morning with a basin of water and set it on the bed so I could wash. "Jim," he would say, "we have to wash your rear-end. We don't want any hemorrhoids." He looked at me so earnestly that I could almost believe he was exactly where he wanted to be, spending his retirement taking care of his grown son.

Jim, You All Right?

I'll never forget that night. When we arrived at the scene a policeman kept my wife on the road so she didn't have to see all the blood and her son spread out on the lawn. But I walked up to Jimmy, and I stayed there a long time while the paramedics worked on him. No parent should ever have to see such a thing. I didn't know if he would live or die. All I knew was that my son was lying in a pool of blood on someone's lawn. What the hell happened?

I visited Jimmy every day when he was in the hospital and rehab. At the time I had a car that was terrible in snow. One day I called and told Jimmy I was coming to see him and he told me to stay home because snow was forecasted. So I sat at Jim's house watching television. But I had this feeling: I just had to go no matter that my son told me to stay home. When I walked through the door in rehab he said, "What are you doing here?"

"I was sitting on the couch. I felt I had to see you."

"If it starts snowing, you're out of here."

"It's a deal."

And it did start snowing, about ten minutes later. A deal's a deal, so I left, but I felt like a million bucks just for the ten minutes I visited.

Often when I visited Jim in rehab we watched television, but usually both of us fell asleep, him in his wheelchair and me in the chair by the bed. The one who woke up later would ask, "What happened in that movie?" and the other would respond, "I don't know, I just woke up too."

It was a great day the day Jim could come home. But it was a scary day too, because I was now the main caregiver for my son. When my kids were growing up I worked six days a week at my gas station. I left home early in the morning before the kids got up, and I usually got home after they had gone to sleep. I wished I could have spent more time with my kids, but that's just the way it was: I needed to be at the station to keep the business going, and I needed to support my family. But forty years later, after Jimmy was hurt, he needed someone to stay with him. My wife Barbara needed to go back to Las Vegas, where we now live part of the year, to take care of some things. So, I was the man for the job. For the foreseeable future, I would be with my son all day and all night.

The hardest thing to do was to put Jim's body brace on. It was a two piece turtle-like shell. Often in the beginning we would laugh when I got Jim out of bed and the brace was all crooked. He would have to lie down and together we would try Take 2. After awhile, like anything else, practice makes perfect and we got it down. Although I always knew my son was very uncomfortable in his brace, I tried to take his mind off it. I knew eventually we both had to get out of the house, so I tried to take Jim to the movies. We got part way to the cinema but the roads were a little slick and Jim got real scared of being hurt again. I didn't want to have my son scared and I knew he'd be thinking of the ride home and wouldn't concentrate on the movie, so I turned around and went back home.

Not long after that it was New Year's Eve. Jimmy and I didn't have any plans; we were going to stay in and take it easy. But I realized I needed to get my prescription filled. It was hard for Jimmy to go out due to all the pain he was in, but he wasn't allowed to stay by himself at this time, so we threw a coat over his back brace, put on his hat and gloves, and off we went. I got my medicine first at Walgreens. After that we decided, what the heck, it's New Year's, let's go out to eat. So we went to the Chinese Buffet. It's one of our favorite places, and it sure beats the meals my son and I had been cooking up. Once we got inside Jimmy took off his jacket. It was only then that we realized he had forgotten to put a shirt or sweater over his back brace.

Man, did the people stare. One little boy in particular kept turning his head and gawking at Jimmy. After a while I leaned over to the little boy's table and said, "That there is one of the original teenage mutant ninja turtles."

The boy stared at Jimmy, sitting there in his turtle shell of a back brace. "Wow," the boy said softly, shaking his head, awestruck.

We all got a good laugh out of that, even the boy's parents.

But it was by no means all laughs. There are things as a caregiver you've just got to do. The first day Jim was back from rehab I got him settled and told him, "Time to wipe your rear-end. No son of mine is getting hemorrhoids or anything else on my watch."

When Jimmy was in bed he couldn't get up to use the bathroom because he didn't have his brace on. So we gave him a urinal bottle to use in the night. Every morning I would dump it. One morning after we had put on his brace and he had gone to the bathroom, he asked me if someone had been using his mouthwash; it seemed like it was disappearing faster than he was using it. I told him I'd been using it each morning to try to freshen up his urinal.

I often had to leave the house to run errands. Since I was just going to town, I always told Jimmy I'd be right back. But it usually didn't work out that way. Most days I'd run into people at the bank or post office or grocery store or gas station who asked about Jimmy, and I'd get talking. But luckily, when I finally got home Jim was usually in the exact same position I'd left him.

Ordinarily I'm a sound sleeper. But when I stayed with Jimmy I was like a mother with a newborn baby. At the slightest sound I would wake up and yell out, "Jim, you all right?" Jimmy would yell back across the hall, "I'm okay." But I usually got up anyway. Jimmy didn't want to bother me, but more often than not he needed my help with shifting to a new position or wanted some water or some medication for pain.

Sometimes I would stand in the doorway and look in at my son, and remember when my son John knocked frantically on our door and told us, "Jimmy's been hurt!", when the doctors told us they were going to induce a coma, when we sat in the hospital room and prayed for Jim to make a turnaround for the better, seeing him with all those machines and tubes coming out of him, talking to him in hopes of him hearing us, applying cold towel compresses on his forehead because he was sweating so much. I would remember the day we arrived at the hospital, a few weeks after he'd been admitted, and saw our son sitting up in a chair for the first time with his braces on. He looked awful and in a lot of pain, but to see him sitting up was like seeing him in a tuxedo.

I would leave Jim's doorway and go back to my bed and listen in the night for any more sounds. Most nights, it wouldn't be long before I'd be yelling again, "Jim, you all right?"
- John Bay

In January 2010, my sister Diana drove my dad and me to see my neck and back doctor. There was a chance I might finally be able to take off my braces. We sat in the waiting room. The doctor was late, so anticipation was building. I felt as nervous as a teenager on a first date. The night before I had dreamed I got my braces off. When I was called in to see the doctor, I handed him the CD of my CAT scans. He loaded it into his computer, then told me my back looked healed enough. He told me my neck looked good, too. He took off my neck brace, then manipulated my neck this way and that.

"Good enough," he said.

He turned to do something on his computer, and then turned back to face me. "Will you take that thing off, please?" he said.

I didn't have to be told twice. I know that body brace saved my life, but I threw it off me like a prisoner would throw off shackles.

A few weeks later, my ribs were still killing me, so my dad drove me to the hospital for x-rays. When the technician called my name I followed him into the x-ray room. He asked me what I was there for, just to be sure we were on the same page. When I told him I had broken 11 ribs, he said, "How did you do that?" I told him I fell into a gully off the side of a road. I wasn't sure I should say more, but I had decided that I would tell my story. And so I told him about the Light and seeing God. He asked me if I would stay a minute, because he wanted one of his colleagues to meet me. He paged her and she came to the room.

"You've got to hear this guy's story," he said to her.

"Make it quick, I've got a lot to do."

"He can't make it quick."

"Then I'll be back in a few."

She went off and did what she needed to do, and returned a few minutes later. I told her what had happened to me. When I told her about God it seemed her feet were lifting off the floor. She got up and closed the door and then sat again beside me. She sat with me for more than ten minutes. It was then I knew that people were hungry to hear about God. I don't know why God gave it to me to do this, but if it is His will, I will do it.

My dad brought me to get my hair cut at the mall. I usually go to one of those drop-in places where you get sent to whoever happens to be available. After I sat down, the hairdresser asked me, "How do you want it done?"

I said, "I used to get it cut shorter, but now I've got a scar that I like to keep covered."

"I hope there's a good story to go along with that scar," she told me jokingly, "not like the stories I hear all the time about people tripping when they were kids and hitting their heads on the coffee table."

"Oh, I've got a story alright."

I told her what had happened to me on Hammertown Road.

"Yeah, that's some story."

"By the way, last time I was here the lady who cut my hair left my bangs long. I was wondering if you could cut them shorter? My hair grows so fast."

"Sir, if you don't mind me saying, after all you've been through, you shouldn't complain too much about a bad haircut."

I was going to say something, but she had already got the point of anything more I might have said.

I finally got to see my kids in February. They came down from Maine with Yanina. Yanina hadn't told them yet about my accident; she felt it best that I do that myself. After Yanina left, the kids and I sat in our usual spots- me in the recliner, and Logan and Lauryn on the couch.

"Your daddy has something to tell you," I said. And I told them about my fall, and how I had climbed out of the ditch, and how I had seen God. I told them about my time in the hospital and rehab. I told them I was lucky to be alive, and that I hoped they understood why we hadn't told them earlier. I could tell from the looks on their faces that Yanina had done the right thing not telling them. I was grateful too that they had come in February, and not around Christmas as originally planned, because now I had my braces off. They hugged me and told me they were glad I was alive. I showed them the comments and the pictures of me in the hospital on the Caring Bridge website. Seeing the pictures helped them realize how badly I had been hurt. After that, for the rest of the week until Yanina returned to pick them up, they watched me out the corners of their eyes. If I made any sounds of pain- a grunt or groan, if I grimaced or had trouble shifting my weight- they would say, "You all right, Daddy?"

What Doesn't Kill You

Jim and I met some years back through his brother John, who has been a friend of mine since around 1997. John came to me asking if I could counsel his brother on some financial matters, because I'm a banker by trade. He told me Jimmy was in some pretty dire straits and needed somebody to talk to. Before then I'd bumped into Jimmy here and there but didn't really know him that well. Jimmy came to see me one evening and disclosed to me that he had himself in a mountain of debt. He didn't make any excuses for it or tell me any of the usual stories that I'm used to hearing about blaming others, including the people who'd lent the money. That's not Jimmy's style. I prodded him a bit, and he shared with me that the debt was primarily due to bills that he'd run up in an effort to take care of his older son, who'd been diagnosed with kidney disease and ultimately passed away as a result of it. He had run up bills taking his son back and forth for dialysis and buying another residence to move to where they could arrange to have dialysis equipment on the premises. There were other problems- like some poor decisions on home financing- but Jimmy had worked hard and spent every dime his family had to achieve an end that was never realized- namely, saving his son's life. I told him that the bankruptcy laws were made for people like him and suggested that he find an attorney and consider filing bankruptcy. But true to form, he told me that he owed the money and that he didn't feel right about bankruptcy. Despite his objections, my advice to him remained the same.

After that, Jimmy and I met often and talked a lot. We became closer friends. My son Alec was killed in an auto accident when he was 14, a week before his 15th birthday, a commonality that Jimmy and I had, both having lost a child and understanding what it's like to go through that, and to be haunted by all the things in life you thought would turn out better, and the struggle to get through it.

One evening I was at home and got a call from Jimmy's brother John. He told me Jimmy had been in a terrible accident, that he had fallen down a ravine a few days ago and was in intensive care. John apologized for not calling me sooner, but told me that he'd pick me up and give me a ride over to the hospital so we could see Jimmy. When I went in the hospital room I have to say it was a horrific sight. Jimmy was lying there with his head all bandaged up and tubes coming out of his mouth. He's a big, strong man, but he'd broken so many bones that it was hard to know whether he was going to pull through.

A few days later, John took me to see the site where Jimmy had fallen, and when I saw it I realized exactly how horrible, or how miraculous, it was what Jimmy had been through. There was a 12 to 14 foot drop onto riprap and jagged rocks. I don't know how he found the strength to climb out of there, with all those broken bones, through the leaves, up a hill, over a log, across a road and onto somebody's lawn to call for help. Being a man of faith, Jimmy believes God chose to save him and spare him that day. And I believe that too, in my own way. My own beliefs are less geared toward any specific religion, but I'm a believer in God and a Higher Power. Somehow, somebody intervened on Jimmy's behalf and gave him the strength to crawl out of there, because there is no way any normal person with those kinds of injuries could do what he did that night. Whatever the reason, God chose not to leave Jimmy Bay to die in a ditch.

It's strange how as our friendship has grown, Jimmy and I realize how many things we have in common and all the different connections we share: Jimmy knowing my son Alec, me finding out that I had known Jimmy's son Robert when he was little, and that I had known Jimmy's ex-wife Yanina before he was married to her because she lived next door to me. I also knew Jimmy's father, Big John, and his mother Barbara; Barbara was a secretary at my son's school, and John was a custodian there. Jimmy was my son's basketball coach. Just funny, how all these threads come together, and you realize that you were meant to be connected, that maybe you always were connected. People with common challenges and common goals and common pain and common natures find each other in this world to help carry each other. Maybe that's what God does: he makes sure there's somebody there with a hand when we need it.

I worry about Jimmy. He gets pretty down sometimes now, mainly due to the limitations placed on him by his injuries. Jimmy's a very bright guy, but due to his skull fracture and some damage to his brain, he often finds himself grasping for words and having difficulty remembering things. He was a big, strong guy with a bright mind, but now he finds himself challenged by the simplest things. But I think he still faces all this with dignity and courage. He's not ever a guy with his hand out; as a matter of fact, he can be a pain in the neck, because even when you want to do something nice for him, something small, like bringing him out to lunch or dinner, he has a hard time accepting that it's okay to lean on some people. The fact of the matter is that much of his life has been a challenge, and he's held himself up most of the way, so I don't see any shame in others helping to hold him up part of the way, too. But that's just one man's opinion.

You meet people who go through their lives virtually unscathed-adversity seems to pass them by; the worst thing that happens to them is a broken ankle. And then you meet people like Jim, people who have been through challenges that no one should have to go through. You've just got to wonder why. I believe- myself having shared some of the lousy things in life that Jim has- that I wouldn't be the same person had it not been for adversity, and I think the same thing is true of Jim. We grow through these things and become better people, and stronger people. That all sounds very cliché, but unfortunately clichés are clichés because they're true. Some subscribe to the statement, 'What doesn't kill you makes you stronger.' But I heard something better, and I choose to believe that it's correct, and that is, 'What doesn't kill you defines you.' And I think that's what all these events in Jimmy's life have done, and that's what the bad things in my own life have done. The pain Jimmy's been though helps him realize compassion and empathy for others. Jimmy is a good man with a good heart, a brave man with a brave soul. He has a very strong sense of right and wrong, and strong religious convictions and beliefs. He didn't deserve any of the things that happened to him, but he accepted them nevertheless, and is working hard to get through all the continuing challenges. He does so with a quiet bravery that might not be noticed at first, but it's there and it's something to be revered.

*   - Geoffrey Talcott*

A few months after I had my braces removed, in April 2010, my cousin Veronica's son Kahliff died suddenly. At that time I was not yet working at all, so I spent most of the days after Kahliff's death at my cousin Rich's house, where family and friends were gathering. The night before the wake and funeral I was awoken at 3 AM. I sat upright in my bed and recited a speech. When the speech was finished, something was said to me: *You will speak at the funeral.* I replied, *Ain't no way I'm speaking at that funeral.*

I went to the wake the following evening and the service was very well attended. At the end of the wake I went up to my cousin and gave her a hug. While we were hugging, Veronica's daughter Sarah rushed up and said that she and her brother Ben were going to say a speech at the funeral. Something nudged me, and before I could stop myself the words were out: "I might say a little something, too."

When I got home I went to bed and tried to sleep. I wasn't sleeping well from all the pain I was still having, but I drifted off. Again at 3 AM I awoke and again the words came. As best I remembered, the same words from the night before. Again I was told I would speak at the funeral. Since my accident I'd been experiencing severe short-term memory loss, so even though I still thought there was not a chance I would be speaking, I thought I'd write the words down. But then I thought, if these are God's words, then there's no need to write them down. I went back to sleep.

My cousin Veronica is the captain of the town rescue squad and very active with the fire company. Kahliff, who was only 5 years old, was always around and was an honorary fire chief. So he was going to receive a fire chief's funeral. There was a procession from the firehouse to the church. Along the route a great many townspeople came out to pay their respects.

Because I was still having trouble walking, we drove and arrived at the church early. At the church, while waiting for the procession to arrive, the Pastor sat down next to me.

"How're you doing?" she asked me.

I told the pastor what I'd lately been telling everyone. "I've been better. And I've been worse."

"I hear you've seen the Light."

"In more ways than one."

When the funeral service began I kept saying to myself, *No way I'm saying a word*.

Sarah and Ben spoke. When they were finished I got that nudge again, this time stronger than before. Without hardly realizing it, I stood up. It was almost like I'd been pushed in the back. I was walking with a cane, and the cane made a distinctive clacking sound, so people knew I was on the move. It was too late to sit back down.

When I reached the altar, I spoke about how a few Saturdays ago I had a tough time sleeping due to the pain I was in, and had been awake all night watching television. My brother called at 8:30 in the morning and asked if I wanted to go to Kahliff's fifth birthday party. I hadn't slept all night and felt exhausted, but I also welcomed the opportunity to get out of the house. After hemming and hawing, I said okay. When we got to the bowling alley for the party, I was looking forward to just watching everyone having fun, but Veronica yelled out, "Jimmy, you're not getting off that easy! Come and keep score." So that's what I did. I was able to spend some wonderful time with my cousin Veronica and her son Kahliff just before their tragedy. And so I told the people gathered there in church that day, think hard when you receive a call. I don't mean only a phone call, like the one I received from my brother John, but more than that, an inner feeling, a nudge, a call you might receive from your conscience or from God. Think twice before you say no to a call like that.

***

Now that I was out of the hospital and rehab, there was one thing I knew I had to do. But it was going to be very difficult. I had to visit my neighbor. I tell everyone that three people saved me that night, along with the doctors and nurses and paramedics, of course: God, my neighbor Indira, and myself. Before the accident I had never had occasion to knock on my neighbor's door. I didn't really know her at all. So it was going to be difficult to get up the courage to go back to the same door where, a few months before, I had knocked hoping someone would answer and help save my life. I didn't have her phone number, and didn't feel I could simply knock and say, *Hi, it's me again, remember last time I was here?* If there were tortured memories, ghosts, of that night still waiting there on her front lawn for me, I imagined they were also there for her. She might not want to see me again. I wanted to set up an appointment: she would know I was coming, and I would be prepared to again see the place I collapsed and nearly bled to death.

But I finally got up the courage to walk over. When I first saw the lawn and the door, the memories and nightmares started flooding back. The steps to that door were almost as tough as those I took on that night months earlier, but I reached the door and knocked. When I did, I was praying Indira wouldn't be there, that maybe someone else would answer the door. It is a small miracle, but my prayer was answered: her daughter answered the door this time. She told me her mom wasn't home. I introduced myself, said I was the one who came to the door that terrible night, and asked for her Mom's phone number. She wrote it down for me. As I walked back to my house, I thought, *God is good.* I simply didn't feel ready to relive those events right then.

I called Indira the next night and we set up an appointment the following day, which was Sunday. I called again right before I walked over to be sure she was in, and she said to come right over. Again the images of that night came rushing into my head when I saw her lawn and door. I had brought a bouquet of flowers for her, an incommensurate measure of thanks for what she had done that night, but at least it was a small gesture of gratitude. She gave me a hug and I think we were both overwhelmed by a feeling of how unbelievable it was for me to be standing there again, months later, not a drop of blood in sight. We sat down and she told me the events of that night from her point of view. She told me she did not sleep at all that night, but I imagine she was being charitable not mentioning all the other nights she might have lost sleep. I realized how it must have been for her to have a person with his skull cracked open, blood streaming down his face, appear at her door one otherwise ordinary night. Even in the hospital, after I had come out of my coma and was able to reflect somewhat on the events of that night, I thought how that poor woman's life would never be the same.

We hardly knew each other, but I felt sure that my bloodied face would be an image she would never forget. I prayed that seeing me now might help her remember me in a better light. As for me, her face that terrible night, haloed in the light from the doorway, was and will forever be, the face of an angel.

Station of the Cross

My dad and mom purchased our family gas station in the Hudson Valley with a partner back in the 1960's. At the time, my dad was commuting about an hour and fifteen minutes north on the Taconic Parkway from our home in Hawthorne, in Westchester County. Anyone who's ever driven on the Taconic will tell you it's not the safest of highways: it's narrow and winding, and there are numerous crossings. On one of those commutes my dad was in an accident that totaled his car; the engine ended up in the front seat and the steering wheel in the backseat. Luckily, my dad wasn't badly hurt. After that, my parents moved us farther upstate so there would be less of a commute. My parents bought out their partner and turned the Sunoco station into a Mobil. We've been running it ever since. At one time there was a fireplace in the station, and my dad would sit and talk to customers for hours. My dad is a good, honest, hardworking man, and if someone came to him for repairs but he thought the car could go a few more miles, he told them so. He did this all the time, to save his customers money, even though his own family was struggling with finances.

When my dad retired, my brother and his wife Mary Ann and I stepped in and took it over. We rented out the mechanic shop and opened a convenience store. We never did get our liquor license- which would have been good for business at a convenience store- but my brother and sister-in-law decided to keep it that way because we had quite a few recovering alcoholics who came to our shop, thankful that it was dry. After a while I had trouble putting in enough money to be an owner so I got out, but I continued to work there as a clerk. Over the years, despite the absence of alcohol at our store, I've often felt like a bartender: people come in for coffee or a lottery ticket or a bag of chips and end up telling you about their lives, their problems, or asking for advice.

We closed the station in 2008 to do some upgrades to the tanks. We had it scheduled to open again in 2009. I was going to run the day-to-day of the landscaping business while John opened up the station. But late in 2009, I fell off Hammertown Road. When we finally opened the station in 2011, it had been closed for nearly three years.

My family has owned the station for more than forty years, and we had built up a loyal customer base. The regulars started to come back.

I recognized the man when he walked in- long blond hair, stocky, wearing sunglasses. He was a customer from years ago. He walked over to the coffee counter and got himself a cup of coffee.

"Great to see you back in business," he said to me.

"Good to be back."

He came to the counter and paid for his coffee. "Why'd it take you so long to re-open, if you don't mind my asking?"

"Well, we had some deaths in the family, and also I was hurt real bad."

He walked toward the door to leave but then stopped. He turned and said, "What happened to you?"

"I fell into a gully and broke 23 bones."

"How'd you get out of there?"

"I climbed out and walked to my neighbor's house."

"With 23 broken bones?"

"You may believe me or not, that's okay, but God helped me out of there too."

He pulled a necklace out from beneath his shirt. A cross.

I told him, "I don't want to hold you up if you have somewhere to be."

"I do have somewhere to be, but now I'm 100% sure that place is right here."

And so we talked for half an hour, just as customers sometimes did with my dad around the fireplace back in the day. We realized we didn't know each other's names, so we introduced ourselves. Pete stayed long enough, listening to me describe my visit from God and the walk to my neighbor's house, that he needed a coffee refill.

As he was leaving, he said, "I can't wait to get in the car and call my wife and tell her about this."

I told him God had told me to tell the story, and that I was trying to write a book about my experience. I asked him if I could describe our conversation in the book. "You can," he said. "As a matter of fact, why don't you write that you made a two-hundred and fifty pound man cry." He lifted up his sunglasses, and there were tears in his eyes.

It was a rainy weekday at the gas station. I was taking care of some bank deposits at the counter when a gentleman came through the doors. I greeted him with a smile and said, "Good morning, kind of wet outside."

"Yeah, it just adds to my pain."

I could tell by the look on his face he wasn't having a good day. I said, "I'm sorry to hear that. What kind of pain do you have?"

He was grimacing as he filled his coffee cup. "It's mostly neck pain. I broke my neck in an accident years ago."

"I know what you're going through. How did it happen?"

"I was in a car accident."

He paused a moment to finish making his coffee. When he came to the counter and paid for his coffee, I said, "I'm real sorry to hear that you're hurting, but hang in there, tomorrow could be a better day."

He got to the door and pushed it open, but then turned around and said, "I never did ask how you know what I'm going through."

I started to tell him briefly about my fall and how I had climbed up out of the gully to get help. He came back inside and stood next to the counter. When I got to the point of talking about God I said, "I don't know if you believe in God or not…"

"I believe in God. You don't have to worry about that."

"I ask out of respect to the person I'm talking to."

And so I told him about seeing the Light and meeting God on Hammertown Road.

"That's an amazing story. It's downright crazy the things you had to do to get help. With that much damage to your body, I have nothing to complain about."

"Sure you do. Everyone deals with pain differently. The difference is that when someone has pain from similar injuries, you can more easily respect what the other person is dealing with. I'm sorry to hold you up. You must have somewhere to be. But that's how I know what you're going through."

"My friend, you're way too humble with all that you've been through."

"I give it all up to God. He has a plan for me and I try to take one day at a time."

We said our goodbyes and out the door he went. I probably made him late, but I have a habit of doing that to people when I start talking about God.

Another customer needed my help out at the pumps, so I went out to help her with her credit card. On the way back into the store I saw a piece of paper on the ground in front of the door. I picked it up and saw it was a receipt from our station.

A few minutes later the man I had been speaking to came back in.

"Did you forget something?"

"I dropped my receipt somewhere and I need it to get reimbursed at work."

"You dropped it by the door and I threw it away, but I'll print you up a new one."

"Thanks a lot for doing that, and thanks too for telling me your story. I was having a really bad day and then I pulled in to this gas station and met you. After hearing all you've been through, it makes everything I'm dealing with easier to bear. The amazing thing is I wasn't going to pull into this station to get gas, but something in my gut told me this is where I had to get gas. I was wondering why I was feeling that way and now I know it was to meet you to hear your story."

All I could say was, "God Bless you my friend and be well."

At the door he said, "Amen."

And that's how so many conversations go nowadays. I sometimes feel there is a cross above the gas station. So many people who come in end up talking to me about God. When I begin to tell my story to people, they always ask, "Who saved you?" I could tell them the paramedics saved me, the ambulance drivers, my doctors and therapists and family and friends, and that would all be true. I could tell them that I saved myself, that somehow I pulled myself up out of that hole and walked toward the light, and that would be true as well. But that wouldn't be the whole truth and nothing but the truth. God let me know He wanted me to tell my story, and so that's what I do. My story wouldn't be complete without God.

I don't preach. If people ask, I tell them I was hurt. If they're still interested, I tell them the short version- that I climbed up out of the pit and walked to my neighbor's house. If they ask more questions, I tell them they might believe me or not, that's okay, but I also saw God. And if they haven't bolted for the door by then, I give them the long version. Some stay for half an hour, even though they have things to do and places to be.

Most people ask lots of questions- about what God looked like, what God sounded like, what God said, how I could be certain it was God. Of course not everyone believes me. Some probably think I'm nuts but are too polite to tell me straight out. I fell 14 feet onto my head that night, so it's only reasonable some might think I was hallucinating or only seeing what I wanted to see. Other people have different doubts. Quite a few people don't believe in God at all. I told my story to one gentleman at the station, and he told me, "I'm sorry to hear about everything that happened to you, but I don't believe in God. Actually, it makes it even more amazing, what you did, crawling up out of there, because you did it yourself without divine intervention." I told him I'd never quite thought of it like that. I respect everyone's opinion, and I'm genuinely curious to hear what people have to say. So I asked him why he didn't believe in God, and he said, "If there was a God, bad things wouldn't happen to good people like you, and good things wouldn't happen to bad people." When I talk about my experience, I hear this often. I know there are entire theologies about this question- the question of pain and evil and suffering in the world- and hundreds of books written about it. I guess it provides the lifeblood for many priests and pastors and reverends. In response to suffering, many of us take some comfort in little sayings: everything happens for a reason; God only gives us as much as we can handle; it's all part of a plan; God had work for my children to do in Heaven. At one time or another, especially since my fall, I've said all of these myself. I've had my doubts; I've questioned myself, and my sanity. And so maybe those little sayings help comfort me. But then I always remember the night I held on for dear life to that log on the side of Hammertown Road. I remember, with a vividness like I could never remember anything else, when God came to me in the Light. And whenever I remember that, all those doubts, all those questions, are answered.

Another day I was working when a customer came in to get gas. I hadn't seen her in a long time. We only knew each other from the station, but Donna was special to me because she helped me a great deal when my son Robert was battling kidney disease. She has kidney disease herself, and she would always give me good advice and cheer me up when things weren't going well with Robert. She was an inspiration to me. She was also very comforting when Robert passed away. My brother had told her I'd been hurt, but she didn't know much more than that. I thought she deserved the long version, so I told her everything. When I told her about all the damage to my body, like everyone else, she cringed. When I told her about seeing God, she said, "I've got goosebumps." She was going to rush home to tell her husband, and asked me to tell him the story when he came in for gas. "I've always believed that people see God," she said, "but until today I've never actually met anyone who saw Him for real." After she left with her coffee, I looked down at my own arms: goosebumps.

Just Ask Jim!

I feel that during the journey of your lifetime, the Lord lets you meet people by his direction and not by coincidence. I feel this way about Jim Bay. I know this now because at times when I would get gas from his station, my spirit would be recharged talking about God's presence in our lives. We would often talk about his son and about how the Lord was helping him cope with kidney problems. This interested me; having had kidney issues, I could relate to what his son was dealing with. And I could see how God was helping me in my life.

Jim and I would frequently talk at length about God's working in our lives. I could see that Jim's belief in God was uplifting and real. Now I know that one of his greatest blessings has been to meet the Lord here on earth. When he told me the story of his fall and the obstacles he had to endure, it was evident that God was protecting him the entire time. All the while Jim told me the story, it hit me how real God is, and that He wants us all to know him in a very personal way. When Jim met the Lord on that log and saw his radiance, I was shivering. I actually know someone now who has seen the Lord.

God was directing Jim all the way up to the log from the ravine. Jim met obstacles along the way and almost died, but God had a bigger plan for him. God always has a bigger and better plan for us than we have for ourselves.

Jim is now a witness for the Lord and is alive to tell his story. It is the same in each of our journeys during life. We all have obstacles and feel like we're not going to make it at times, but with God's help we can overcome every challenge. Just ask Jim!

- Donna Philipbar

A day at the gas station. I had to go into the office to do a little paperwork. Before I left the counter area I looked out to see if anyone was at the pumps. Only an older gentleman pumping his gas. So I decided it would be safe for me to go into the office. Usually when I'm in the office I leave the door slightly opened so I can hear the ring of the door

107

if someone comes in. After I'd been in the office a bit, I heard the door ring, so I got up and stepped out into the store area.

It was the older man who had been pumping gas. "Sorry," he said. "I didn't mean to take you away from what you were doing."

"Don't worry about that. My first job is to take care of customers."

"I guess you got a point there."

He walked around the aisles for a few minutes then came to the counter to pay for his things.

"Why was this place closed for so long? It was a few years, wasn't it?"

"Yes, almost three years."

"How come so long?"

"My brother had new tanks put in. And on top of that, I got hurt real bad and couldn't work for a while."

"What happened to you?"

Like I did with most people, I told him the quick version. I also told him about meeting God.

When I was finished telling him the story, he said, "I believe you one hundred percent, and I'll tell you why. Do you have a minute?"

I'm usually the one who asks that question, so I couldn't help but smile. "I've got all day. At least until closing time anyway."

"This is a true story that happened when I was younger. I was working in New York City at the time. I usually took the subway and walked to my office. On this day I was on the sidewalk in front of my building when I had the most severe pain in my chest. I managed to get over to a bench to sit down. I couldn't speak and the pain was getting worse. Just then a colleague of mine walked by and said, 'You'll be late for work if you don't start moving.' I was able to look up at him and I guess he could tell I was in big trouble. He went running down the block to a phone booth. No cell phones in those days. As I was saying, he went off down the sidewalk, and I looked after him. And there, right on the sidewalk, right in the street, in New York City, was the most beautiful glowing light shining from that direction. It was no ordinary light. It was illuminating me, like a sunrise or something. I heard a voice, 'Hey, mister, are you all right?' I was able turn my head in the direction of the voice and I could see a paramedic in an ambulance that had been passing by. All I could do was shake my head and his partner parked the ambulance. They came running to help me and took me to the hospital, where I had surgery for a heart attack. The doctors told me afterwards that if those paramedics had not been passing by at that moment I would have died on that bench. I also found out that my colleague who ran for the phone booth hadn't made it yet when the ambulance showed up. So you see, I've had my own God experience, so I know exactly where you're coming from."

"What a story."

"You have one amazing story, too, and as you already know it's a miracle that you're here today to tell it."

And so there we were, two men who had seen the Light, who had been granted life after being so close to death. And I couldn't help but wonder- How many others? How many other men and women and children who walked through the ringing doors of my gas station had a story to tell, a story like mine?

A man started stopping at the gas station early in the morning. After a few visits he saw me walking with my cane. While he was paying for his coffee, he asked, "Did you hurt your leg?"

"That might be about the only part of my body I didn't hurt. I got hurt pretty bad a few years ago. Since then I have very bad dizzy spells, so I walk with a cane as a precaution to stop me from falling."

"How did you get hurt, if you don't mind my asking?"

Like I did with everyone, I told him the quick version.

A few days later he came back in and we picked up where we left off. "By the way," he said, "my name is Jim."

"Thank God, finally a name I can remember."

"Why do you say that?"

"Because Jim is *my* name. With my brain injury I'm very forgetful, but I don't usually forget my own name."

We both had a good laugh.

The following week he came back in for coffee. When I saw him come through the door I said, "Good morning, Jim."

He said, "Good morning, Jim."

We had another laugh and started talking. I always tried to make it short with him each morning, because he had a bit of a ride to work and was usually cutting it close. But this morning we ended up chatting longer then we should have. He looked at the clock and told me he had to run.

"I'm sorry for making you late, Jim. I have a habit of doing that when people get me talking about God."

The next morning Jim came by the station again. "Good morning Jim," he said. "I can't stay long but I have something to tell you."

"Morning to you Jim, and I'm all ears. I promise I won't talk."

He laughed as he filled up his coffee and then came over to the counter and paid. "You know how I ended up staying later then I should have yesterday morning?"

"I sure do. I'm awfully sorry about that."

"Well, don't be."

"Why not?"

"We talked about God so long yesterday morning it kept me from getting in to a bad accident."

"What do you mean?"

"Because I left here later than I should have, I drove up on a car accident that had just happened. If I didn't stay and talk about God with you, I might have been involved in the accident. I just wanted to say thanks for holding me up yesterday. But I don't want to push my luck and be late for work again, so I'd better get going today."

"I don't think luck had anything to do with it, Jim. Take it from me, it was God, and he has a plan for all of us."

Been Better, Been Worse

I'm a changed man. My friend Domenica asked my daughter Lauryn if her dad was different after his accident. She said, "Yeah, he walks with a cane, he stutters, he has a scar on his head and he forgets things." Though my broken bones have healed, I have aches and pains now in places I didn't know it was possible to have aches and pains. In cold weather, especially, I'm never without pain. There are days I struggle to get out of bed. My entire body often throbs like a headache. I have headaches all the time. I often get dizzy, and though I've received balance therapy to help me with the dizziness, I still walk with a cane when necessary for support. Sometimes when I get dizzy, I fall. This frightens me more than anything, since the doctors told me I should never fall on my head again. My memory isn't what it used to be: I forget things if I don't write them down. I sometimes stutter my words now, and occasionally say the wrong word- I might say *bat* when what I want to say is *hat*. Sometimes I forget words, and gaping holes open up in my conversations as I wrack my brain trying to find the word for what I want to say. More often than not it's the simplest little word, but I simply can't remember it.

I have nightmares where I'm falling, free-fall, the rush of air around my body, and I know the crunch is coming. When my head hits the rocks I wake up. I often wake up feeling more tired than when I went to bed. I have three vertebrae in my thoracic region that healed in a crushed position. There is no surgery that can help, so I have to live with the pain.

I'm still afraid to go to the spot I fell and look down into that ravine. I'm not sure I'll ever be able to do that.

I went back to work as a light-duty landscaper. But because there is little that is light-duty about landscaping, the experiment didn't last long. When I lost my disability insurance, my brother and I talked and decided that, to be fair to the landscaping business, I would take less pay and contribute as best I could. I tried to ride the tractor, but every bump rattled my already hurting bones. I used to take great pride in building beautiful stone walls and patios, but I found myself holding ladders, fetching tools for the guys, or weeding. Even bending over or squatting while weeding killed me. My body isn't capable of the physical labor anymore. And so now I work as a clerk at my family's gas station.

Sometimes my life feels like a tennis match, the ball bouncing back and forth between two sides: on one- I feel it a miracle to be here at all; on the other- it hurts to be me. I wake up in pain, go through the day in pain, and go to sleep at night in pain. I know many people live with chronic pain, and many have it much worse than I do, but still my emotions go back and forth, up and down.

And then there is memory. Whenever the Mets play the Yankees, I remember my baby James, because the day my son died I listened to the recap of that day's game on the ride home from the hospital. And every time I see a boat- maybe someone is hauling one down to the Hudson River, or maybe I see one on television- I remember my son Robert, because when I received the call the day he died I was about to go for a ride aboard my friend Brian's boat. And so simple things, things other people might not think twice about- a ballgame, a boat- are forever transformed in my memory. Just so, there are things that remind me all the time of my fall. Whenever I hear a helicopter now I remember the trauma unit, listening to all the choppers taking off and landing. Whenever I pass over a bridge I remember where I fell. Whenever I see an ambulance, a firetruck, hear a siren, whenever I see anyone wearing a brace or using a cane, on November 15, on Thanksgiving, Christmas Eve, in my nightmares, I remember. A hundred little things throughout the day: I remember.

Not Like We Were Before

I first met Jimmy and his family about 15 years ago when I moved to this area. I became close with his father first, when I brought him some things for a septic tank one time from my job. Then I met Jimmy and John. I used to spend my mornings before I went to work talking with them at the gas station. Over time, Jimmy and I became closer, and I admired him because he was a strong man- strong in family values, strong in faith. And his faith was being tested a lot when I first met him. He had lost a baby, and one of his sons was sick and needed a kidney transplant, and that son never recovered after the transplant and eventually passed away. I felt so bad for Jimmy, but you could see it in his eyes- no matter how much was put on his plate, his faith was strong enough to get him by. I was amazed by that; I couldn't even imagine losing a child, let alone two.

And then when his accident occurred, and his brother John first talked to me about it, and I read about it and kept up with his progress on Caring Bridge, it tested my faith, too. Why was God putting so much on his plate? The man had endured so much suffering losing his children, and now physically he had taken the beating of his life in that fall. But God gave him the strength to crawl out of that hole and across the road. You have to say it must be for a purpose. Maybe it is his lot in life to speak the word.

I know how tough it is what he's going through physically because I endured a similar accident: I was hit on a motorcycle and was in the hospital for 7 months, almost lost a leg, and it took me a year before I could even try to walk again with a walker. So I have some idea what it's like. We both suffer physical pain, and more than that we suffer the frustration of not being able to do what we used to do.

113

We talk about these things a lot, me and Jimmy, when I stop in at the gas station. He's got an amazing little sparkle in his eye. You're never going to keep him down. The pain isn't going to keep him down, though now and then he'll talk about it and moan about it- we both do- but he doesn't let it stop him. The only thing that gets us by, and Jimmy reinforced this for me, is our faith in God. He didn't give up, he didn't roll himself up in a ball and say that's it, I can't take it anymore. He could have let his life go many different ways, yet his faith helped him not get down on himself. He picked himself up, literally and spiritually.

I just hope that the pain eventually stops, because I'll tell you, that's one of the hardest things to endure, to keep your chin up and to smile despite the pain. But he does it every day. He amazes me; he takes it and accepts it. I wish I could accept my pain sometimes the way Jimmy does, but sometimes I question God- Why do I have so much pain after all these years? I guess Jimmy does too, sometimes. Neither of us will ever be like we were before, but there are ways to work around that to be able to do the things you want to do. And if anybody can do it, it's Jimmy. I've seen Jimmy's faith and good nature bring so many people to open up to their faith too. Maybe they don't even know it yet, but they are learning from Jimmy.

* - Dominic Vigna*

In June 2011 I was diagnosed with post-traumatic Meniere's Disease. Ever since my fall I had been experiencing dizzy spells, ranging from momentary unsteadiness on my feet to rooms spinning wildly; several times, I had fainted. I had also, over that time, lost some hearing in my left ear. These are the classic symptoms of Meniere's Disease, in my case caused by the blow to my head from the fall into the culvert. When the audiologist gave me the diagnosis, I experienced momentary confusion- "*What disease?*"- and some trepidation, but also relief that I finally had an explanation for my dizziness and hearing loss.

Due to the Meniere's diagnosis, I was becoming increasingly worried about retaining my driver's license. I received a renewal form in the mail, and one of the questions related to dizziness. My ear, nose and throat doctor filled out the appropriate forms, and we sent the renewal off to the Department of Motor Vehicles in Albany. But I was behind schedule. My dad had asked me about my renewal many months previously, but like most things nowadays, if I don't do it immediately, I forget it. So on midnight of July 21, my birthday, we had not yet received the renewal in the mail and, without a valid license, I officially could no longer drive. It was a strange feeling being without a driver's license. I had to rely on my parents to pick me up at my house and drive me to the gas station to work, and then drive me home again at the day's end. Standing there in my driveway, waiting for my parents to pick me up, I felt like a kid again, waiting for the schoolbus. It was only an intimation of what awaits me- awaits us all, I guess- as we get too sick or too old to drive. But the renewal came only a week later.

I got a ride to the DMV. When I presented my paperwork, including the medical release form, the woman at the counter asked me about Meniere's Disease. She, like me only a few months before, had never heard of it. I gave her the short version- telling her that the Meniere's had been caused by a bad fall. She asked lots of questions, so eventually we got around to the Light and God. She processed my renewal, and I thanked her for her help. "No," she said, "thank *you* for telling me your story. I still have goosebumps." When I drove, later that day, I felt like I had just passed my driver's test for the first time as a sixteen year-old. And so to my list of little everyday miracles- taking a hot shower, getting out of bed whenever I want because I don't need to wear a back brace- I add being able to drive.

A year after my accident, I went to see a neuropsychologist. I knew well enough that I was having trouble with my thinking after my accident. I used to be one of the sharper pencils in the box- I did pretty well in high school and in college- but now I felt like one of the duller ones. One of the first tests at the neuropsychologist's office was a block test: each block is half red and half white, and you've got to copy a picture by building with the blocks. I felt like a little boy on the floor of his room, surrounded by letter blocks. But the more blocks it took to make a picture the worse I did, until when we reached nine blocks I couldn't make a picture at all. I exceeded the allotted time, but the sympathetic doctor let me finish to prove to myself I could do it.

From Neuropsychological Evaluation 12/14/2010
History:

Mr. Bay continues to complain of short-term memory loss, persistent ringing in his ears, persistent headaches, neck pain, ongoing dizziness, unexpected mood changes, persistent but unexplainable fatigue, speech anomalies, which include word finding and word/letter substitutions in known words. Mr. Bay also complains of variability in his vocal timbre, stuttering and what might be described as neologisms. He describes an unusual variability in his rate of speech, poor attention and inadequate concentration and personality changes. Mr. Bay complains of an increased level of irritability, angry outbursts and periods of depression, even though he considers himself fortunate to be alive.

Mr. Bay's verbal reasoning abilities are in the average range when compared to his peers. Mr. Bay's ability to sustain attention, concentrate, and exert mental control is in the low average range. Mr. Bay's ability in processing simple or routine visual material without making errors is in the extremely low range when compared with his peers. Mr. Bay's memory functioning is variable, falling in the average to low average range. Mr. Bay's ability to process information has been confounded by processing speed deficits, which is in stark contrast to his premorbid skills. Premorbidly, Mr. Bay's functioning was clearly in the average to high average ranges.

I may not be able to think straight after my fall, but none of that sounded all that good to me.

***

116

At one of my neurologist visits, the waiting room was full, and a few of us got to talking. Eventually it was down to me and an older couple. The husband asked me why I was there, and I gave him the short version. As I always do, I said, "I don't know if you'll believe me or not, but this is what happened." And I told them how I had seen God. Later, I told them how I was hoping to write a book about my experience. The wife asked me immediately for the title of the book. "Remember that title," she said to her husband, "and don't you forget it." They were called in to see the doctor, and after they came out I was next. But before I walked in, the wife took me by the arm: "I can't wait to read your book. I hope it gets published. Here's my name and number. You call me if that book gets published." After my appointment, I walked out to the car where my dad was waiting. I told him about the neurology tests. And I said, "If my book ever gets published, we've sold our first copy."

When I go shopping, I often give money to a cashier and get distracted by something- a phone call or a conversation- and I forget how much money I've given. They could tell me I hadn't given enough, or give me back a few pennies change when I was owed $20 and I wouldn't know the difference. What I try to do now is to give as close to the exact change as possible. Luckily, no one has cheated me yet. This forgetfulness about money has become something of a problem in the gas station, where *I'm* the cashier. My mom long ago taught me from her days working at Woolworths that you never put what people have given you into your cash drawer until the transaction is finished. So now what happens more than I care to admit is I give a customer their change, and then offer them as well the money they gave me that's still in my hand. Luckily, no one has accepted the money yet.

Monday, November 23, 2009

Jimmy,

Not only so, but we also rejoice in our sufferings, because we know that suffering produces perseverance; perseverance, character; and character, hope. And hope does not disappoint us, because

God has poured out his love into our hearts by the Holy Spirit, whom he has given us. Romans 5:3-5

Keeping you in our prayers and if there is anything anyone needs please let us know.

God bless...Bob, Sandy, Zach and Rebekah K.

I'm not sure I can rejoice in my sufferings, as St. Paul recommends, but I'm slowly making peace with all this. I know I will probably never be able to go on long walks again. My work life is forever changed. I'm terrified of heights; I'm especially afraid of falling again. People who know I've been hurt often ask me, "How're you doing now?" I never tell them "Fine, thanks" because that wouldn't be true. But I also don't want to say, "Well, let me tell you..." because I'd have to go into more detail than the person probably wanted. I know people are concerned, but most ask just to be polite. So nowadays I always say, "Been better, been worse" and that seems to work well enough.

Sometimes, when I'm feeling sorry for myself, I think of my son Robert, and all the things he had trouble doing because of his kidney disease, and of all the things he will never be able to do because he is no longer here to do them. And then I realize I have no right to feel sorry for myself. God has kept me alive, and each morning brings a new day, a day in which anything, absolutely anything, might happen.

During his senior year in high school, Robert decided he wanted to be a mechanic. He was determined to move ahead with his life despite the need for dialysis. He was accepted at a vocational college near where Yanina and I and Logan and Lauryn would be starting a new chapter in our lives in Arizona. And so before we moved to Arizona, I took Robert to Pennsylvania for mechanic school orientation. Though three or four hours away from our home in New York State, this was the closest place for orientation. We rode and listened to the radio. On one talk show there was a guest from the future who had called into the station and said he had only 30 minutes to talk because he needed to return to his own time. The host talked to the man from the future like he believed his every word. Robert and I got

118

to talking then, about time travel and the future. We had some good laughs. Of course neither of us knew our own future, that Robert would be dead within the year. Now, those three or four hours in the car seem precious beyond compare to me. There really is no future-there is only this moment. For the rest of my life, I will try to remember that.

I sometimes think about the things my sons never got to do in life. I guess all parents who lose children think about that now and then. James Ulysses only lived 10 days, but I sometimes wonder who he would have turned out to be, what his interests would have been. Robert never got his driver's license, which for a teenager, of course, is a very big deal. And Robert never had a girlfriend. We often joked about how sexy he looked with the tube coming out his abdomen. He laughed about it quite a bit, but I wonder how he felt inside.

But Robert did get to do one thing that not many people ever experience. When we moved out to Arizona for a fresh start, our possessions were to be sent out by truck, and our family would be driving cross-country. We had one car and five people; there wasn't room for luggage, let alone all the dialysis equipment. Robert needed to do dialysis every day. How to get Robert out to Arizona? Luckily, my cousin, who lives in Las Vegas, heard about our dilemma and incredibly offered to fly Robert out to Vegas in a private jet. It was decided my mom would fly with Robert.

Yanina and the kids and I set off in our car. Robert's brother, Jon, was staying in New York for college. A few days later, Robert and my mom were supposed to get a ride to the airport, but the ride never came. So a friend of my mom's drove them to the airport. They were four hours late, but since they were the only passengers the jet was there waiting for them. I guess it was then they realized how special the day was going to be. When they got aboard, they ordered food. Robert had a sandwich, and my mom had a salad and jumbo shrimp. But Robert kept eyeing those shrimp, and he ended up eating most of my mom's lunch. Needless to say, they flew in style.

So Robert missed out on some things in life, but he got to experience something his old man never has, and is never likely to.

Robert's new apartment in Avondale was a 2 hour drive from us, so it was more difficult to help him with his dialysis. While in Arizona he was admitted to hospital a few more times. Nine months after moving to Arizona, Yanina found Robert dead on his kitchen floor.

When we cleaned out our son's apartment, we found a journal Robert had been keeping. My wife and I didn't read it. We decided to give it to Jon.

From Robert's journal:
4-23-2004
I don't feel as angry inside as I used to. Even though I'm afraid it hasn't faded from me, I'm certain now that I'll never lose control of myself again.

5-28-05
I used to think popularity in school would be the best. Then illness hit me. At first, I thought I'd be well again, but Fate it seems had other plans.

I forget what day it is
Soon I'll be in Arizona. My plan is to first go to school and learn, then become a success. When I'm older, but not too old, like 40 to 50, I'll travel to Japan, China, India and Europe.

After we moved to Arizona, after a stressful morning of job-hunting, I drove up to see Robert. Neither Yanina nor I had a job at the time, and money was tight, but I wanted to buy a coat for my son. We got a nice coat and had lunch together. To this day, when I reflect back on my life, one of the best things I ever did was buy a jacket for my son that day.

A few weeks before Robert died he came to visit Yanina and me for the weekend. He seemed to have lost most of his appetite, but at

120

the time it didn't seem like enough of a sign to become alarmed. Later, after Robert's death, I beat myself up pretty good: there were times when I was so upset at myself, threw so many punches my way, that I felt like I'd been through 15 rounds. If only I had realized what was going on, Robert might still be alive. It has taken some time, but I see now that no matter what we did, things might have turned out the same, or different, or better or worse. The only one who knows is God.

My son Robert faced far worse than I ever did. Death stared me in the face for a week or two. For Robert, death was his ever-present companion. He faced the possibility on a daily basis. Something might go wrong with his dialysis, or his body would stop responding well to the treatment. Or maybe some of the many medications he was taking might make him even sicker. When he finally did meet death, I'd like to believe that he did so unafraid, that he and death were already so well acquainted that they simply shook hands, nodded and walked off together into the night. But to this day I wonder what my stepson was thinking as he fell to his kitchen floor.

I fell 14 feet and lived. Robert fell to his floor and died. It does not seem right. It does not seem fair. There is so much more he could have experienced in the world, so much he could have done. But I give it up to God.

I wanted to go back to my rehab unit a year after my discharge for a visit. But because I often get dizzy, I have trouble driving. I wasn't sure I should go. But I felt a nudge from God. On the drive there I prayed I would get the chance to see my old friend Gayle. Then again, I prayed I wouldn't see her, since that would mean she had managed to get out of rehab and finally go home. When I arrived, I visited with some of the nurses and therapists. And then I walked down the hall toward a woman sitting in a wheelchair. It wasn't Gayle, and I felt hopeful that she might have gone home. But I was told she had been moved up to the third floor, which is a floor for more permanent residents. When I got upstairs, I walked down the hall and there she was, more or less in the same spot by the nurse's station, only one floor up. Without my body brace she didn't recognize me at first. But when I got closer she said, "I've been praying to God that you would visit. And here you are."

"Here I am," I said.

"You look better than the last time I saw you."

She always said that.

As I so often did, I thought again of Robert. He was a teenager and looked fit. You would never guess by looking at him that he had kidney disease or a tube sticking out his abdomen. Everyone treated him like he was completely healthy. Our family sometimes went on picnics or to the beach or other outings with friends, and everyone would wonder why Robert wasn't joining in all the activities. When we told them about Robert's condition, they understood.

As it was with Robert, so it was with me. I wished I felt as good as I looked.

Enough That You Are Here

I will be honest- I have not wanted to go back down these roads, not wanted to recall or recount everything or anything about Jimmy's accident. It's taken me some time to do.

Jimmy is one of those rare people: what you see is what you get. Jimmy brings peace. He is one of the blessed peacemakers. He will avoid confrontation and conflict, even to his own detriment, in order to sustain peace. He is not a fighter. And yet, he is strong. I've no doubt he willed himself with sheer strength and determination to climb out of that gully with a broken neck. To die. And I know, in what he thought were his final moments of life, in his dying, that he wanted to spare a stranger what he could not spare Yanina; he knew all too well the great impact on his wife, the mother, finding her son four days after his death. He did not want his death to be like that.

Jimmy was my personal angel during very difficult years- in my first marriage, through my divorce, my father's terminal illness and death, and my meeting and falling in love with my second husband Kevin. On my wedding day, Jimmy was late. He was off to the hospital in Albany (again) with Robert. But he came. Things were winding down, but there he was on the "dance floor" (the house deck). He was there and I danced with Jimmy on my wedding day. Jimmy and I have a very long history of dancing! Oh, too many times and places to tell. He's been my dancing partner for many years.

In 1995, my husband and I transitioned from Okinawa and the Marine Corps to civilian life in Pine Plains. It was tough. First person I see? Jimmy. I left my car and luggage at his house. He fed me. He helped me rent a house, he welcomed me back from Oki, he embraced me and my kids.

I remember once my stepfather asked Jimmy to help him find the gold St. Christopher's medal he'd been given as a 1ˢᵗ marriage anniversary present. He'd lost that medal very soon after he received it, and it had been missing for more than twenty years. My stepfather showed Jimmy where he had been working the day he lost the medal, then went inside the house for something, saying he'd be right back. Jimmy started his metal-detector and started sweeping the area. After only five minutes of searching, he found that medal, looking almost as new as the day it was lost. My stepfather came back outside. "Hold out your hand," Jimmy said to him, and dropped that medal in his hand. My stepfather was shaken. His eyes teared up. He offered Jimmy money, but Jimmy said the look on his face was payment enough.

When my father was dying and I couldn't come to grips that it was inevitable, Jimmy told me, "To be on earth is a miracle. Doesn't matter how many days you are here- it is enough that you are here. Your dad is 72, baby James was 10 days. Doesn't matter. Being alive on earth affects others- the love you bring, the love they have for you, the connections. It makes a difference. Time is nothing to God." And that was before he saw God.

Hammertown Road- I have a memory, though Jimmy does not. In 10ᵗʰ grade when I was living in New York City with my dad, I came back to Pine Plains for the summer. Jimmy was painting a house on Hammertown Road. I don't know why he was painting- a job per-

haps? I don't know whose house it was. But there was white paint. And what do teenagers do with paint? We painted each other. In between laughs, he told me to come home to Pine Plains. And in the years since, I've learned "home" really is here- these roads, this community, these people, these friends, our life, these memories, these trees. Yes, Hammertown Road, 1982. We could never have foreseen that nearly 30 years later, on Hammertown Road...

I have spoken to Jimmy's brother John maybe three times in my life. That night I came home late, maybe 1 or 2 in the morning. I see that John called my house phone- kind of late, maybe 11pm? That's odd. I have no idea why John would call me. I'm curious and can't get my mind off it. Too late to call him, no message, but I can't shake wondering why he called. I go upstairs to put my purse and things away and see my cell phone has a message. I don't ordinarily carry my cell around- it was plugged in by my bed. Now I recognize John's number from having seen it a moment ago. When I hear his message, his voice isn't right. He tells me to call him, no matter the time. I don't want to call him, but I have to. I don't want to think Jimmy is dead but I'm terrified he is. If I don't call John, I won't know. Still, it won't change things- whether I know or not. Whatever is happening or happened- it did so.

So I call. And John talks for more than an hour. I am numb. With each word, heaviness moves deeper into my heart. I can't say anything encouraging. I have no idea- will he die tonight? Did he die ten minutes ago? How much pain is he in? What do I pray? I don't want him to suffer, I don't want to let go, this isn't about me, this should be about Jimmy, God forgive me, help me pray the right way. What the hell happened? A stranger? Someone tried to kill Jimmy? Must be. Jimmy is a walker. He doesn't fall off roads. Jimmy's conscientious, he's safe (I know this from years of running with him), I know how he conducts himself while out jogging and walking. Somebody (WHO?), some bastard must have tried to run him off the road! Hit and run? I know, beyond any shadow of any doubt, Jimmy did not try to kill himself. I know everything that's happened in his life, all the pain and children dying and missing the kids in Maine, Jimmy would not kill himself then, or now, not ever. And actually, Jimmy's been kind of better lately; yes he misses the kids, but he's managing and adjusting. He and I are making plans to go to Maine. So what happened? I wait until morning. In agony.

At first light my husband Kevin goes to the scene of the accident. He comes home and tells me the height and depth of the gully, how it is not humanly possible Jimmy could climb out of there. A person would have trouble climbing out of there healthy, let alone injured. Kevin tells me something extraordinary happened there. Something miraculous happened with Jimmy.

I have to see him. Kevin takes me to the hospital. As we walk in we see Mr. Bay. He tells Kevin, "You need to go with her". Seeing Jimmy in the hospital bed was possibly worse than seeing him dead. At least with dead people you see peace. I honestly don't know if I wanted him to die for relief from this, because I love him that much. Death was in the room. I wondered, So why doesn't he die? What's keeping him alive? There he was all broken. I felt sick, but not because of the pain he was in. (I don't want him to be in pain, still, let him have the pain if he'll recover- but how can he recover from this?) It was the "mangledness." He was mangled. He was broken, mangled and suffering. I had no more thoughts. I had no more feeling.

Mrs. Bay was there. Normally she's very comforting, but her pain was so great and so obvious that it only made for more devastation. I stood by him and was afraid to actually touch him. I never said a word. I didn't cry for fear he'd know, and I didn't want him to think I thought he was dying in case there was a chance he could live. I didn't want him to give up. Kevin talked. Kevin was a rock. He held Jimmy's hand and Jimmy held his hand. He did. In his broken mangled state, he held Kevin's hand. I saw it. I did what was rising up in me to do. I leaned in, all the tubes, the devices, the shattered bones (every one of them! All broken!) I put my hand on his chest and felt his heartbeat. Not goodbye, not stay, not any huge thought- I wanted to put my hand on his chest, and somehow empty my heart to his. I wanted him to know I loved him. Mrs. Bay got nervous and cautioned me to be careful, don't hurt him. Maybe she was right; breathing on him seemed like it would hurt him. But I thought how the hell could a person possibly feel any more pain than he's feeling now? I kissed him. And I left. I never went back.

There were times I was ashamed and felt bad I didn't go back, but I also knew peace by not going. I can't explain this, it might not make sense, and it might sound very bad on my part, but it's the truth. I couldn't go. I knew I had to pray earnestly for him. I did. I did it where I was quiet and still. After I left the hospital I never changed my mind- I did not want him to die, I did not pray for his suffering to end through death, I prayed he'd get stronger, be well and recover. Every day my prayer became clearer and stronger.

I talked to Yanina, and those talks helped. One day it was time for me to go see him. Just like that. I was at work and knew I would leave work to go to him. Yanina called me just as I was leaving. I told her I was on my way to the hospital, but she told me he was in transit to rehab. She also told me he couldn't have any visitors for now. I felt at peace; I knew he was on his way. I just had to wait. From that point on his sister Diana kept me updated on his progress.

I knew the day to see him would happen when it was supposed to, and it did. I saw him at Veronica's son's funeral. This was a funeral beyond tragic. There was no comfort to offer. But as I made my way through the line, there in a chair sat my friend Jimmy. Oh, he looked wonderful to me. He was in a suit but it wasn't the suit that made him look so good. It was just him. He saw me, he brightened, he kissed me and he said like he always does, "there's my girl." He told the man sitting next to him, "She's my best friend." And me and Jimmy were us again. He made it.

- Domenica Biro

12

A Miracle from Day One

My cousin Veronica, the captain of the town rescue squad, called and told me that every year the company chooses one emergency call and honors the responders with a banquet. This year, the call was mine. She invited me to attend. I knew it wouldn't be easy to sit and listen. I have difficulty sitting for any length of time, but more than that, the events of that night are still raw and painful for me. I still haven't walked down Hammertown Road to see where I fell. And since my accident I'd heard some stories about that night. One person at the scene said I was the toughest SOB he'd ever seen to survive that fall. Zach Koch, an EMT, told his father, Bob: "If you're going to pray tonight, pray for Jim Bay. If he dies, it will be from loss of blood." I wasn't sure I was up for listening to more.

But in early 2011, on a crisp winter's night, my parents drove me to the restaurant where the awards ceremony was to be held. When we arrived, we were ushered through a great crowd of people, some of whom I knew from the firehouse, to our table. Mike, one of the emergency responders, got up to say a few words about the night of November 15,

2009. I learned for the first time that nine people were on the scene that night. When it was my turn, I got up and walked to the front, limping and walking with my cane in hand, to a standing ovation from more than one hundred people. I was so choked up that I couldn't speak. Instead I shook hands and handed out the awards to nine good people who helped save my life.

Later, I said to my cousin Veronica, "Why a standing ovation? If anyone deserves applause it's them, not me."

"Why?" she said. "Unfortunately, many years the person we're honoring is no longer around to hand out the awards. But you're here, and that's a miracle."

For a few years after my accident I needed to see lots of doctors. Though it brought back some painful memories, I sometimes needed to go to Saint Francis Hospital. On one visit, after I'd seen my doctors, I met a young man in the elevator who looked like a doctor.

"How's your day going?" I asked him.

"Done for the day," he said.

"I sure have spent some time in this place."

"You worked here?"

"No, I was a patient in the trauma unit."

"If you don't mind telling me, what happened to you? Why were you here?"

We were both on our way home, but after we walked out from the elevator we stopped in the lobby. I told him about my fall and how many bones I broke and about the other damage to my body.

"And you're walking?"

"It's a miracle to be alive let alone to be walking."

"There's no doubt about that. Something special must have happened that night."

And I knew I needed to tell him about God.

While I was telling him the story a woman who worked at the hospital walked through the lobby and said good bye to him, that it was her last day to work at the hospital. He said it was his last day there, too.

"What do you do here?"

"I'm an intern. I'm on my way back to school."

"What are you studying?"

"Physical therapy. Actually, for the rest of my career, I can inspire all my patients by telling them that I once met a guy while I was an intern who had 26 fractures, 13 in his back and neck. *And* he was walking. If he could do it, so can you."

A warm late-autumn Sunday in November, 2012, maybe the last chance I would have to go metal-detecting before the ground froze for the winter. I got my metal-detecting gear ready for when I came home from church. I went to church and sat in my usual pew in the back. Part of me was listening to Pastor Greg, but another part of me was fantasizing about metal-detecting. I couldn't wait to get out there and see what I might find.

But then I got a nudge. The sort of nudge I'd been noticing frequently since my fall; the sort of nudge that was difficult to ignore.

On Friday the week before, my niece Jenesis had given birth to a baby girl they named Elliot. And so, since my niece Cassandra had given birth a few months earlier, for the second time in less than a year I was a great-uncle.

The voice told me to change my plans, told me I should go to the hospital to see Jenesis, her husband Chris and their baby. I wanted to go metal-detecting. For most of the service I debated. But I'd learned something in the years since my accident: don't ignore a call. And so I decided to go to the hospital.

After the service, I sent a text to my brother to ask if Jenesis and the baby were still in the hospital. He told me they weren't supposed to be, but the baby had jaundice so they needed to stay an extra day. Luck? I wasn't so sure.

Half an hour later I arrived at Northern Dutchess Hospital in Rhinebeck, the same hospital where my children Logan and Lauryn and little James were born. As I walked through the doors, my mind was flooded with memories.

After our sweet baby James died, Yanina and I decided to try one more time for another child. Yanina was soon pregnant again, but a few months into the pregnancy she suffered a miscarriage. We were devastated again, and after this our marriage began to fray at the edges. We had difficulty being intimate. But we both still wanted another child. Yanina and I went to see her gynecologist. He told us despite the miscarriage and the premature birth of baby James, there was no reason why we couldn't try again. Like a fortune-teller, he even told us the exact date we should have sex in order for Yanina to get pregnant again. We were skeptical of the date, but we both went home remembering it.

When the date came we tried being nonchalant but we both knew what we had to do. There were three kids in the house, one of whom was a toddler, so it was hard to find time to be alone. But we finally found a few minutes. There was about as much pleasure in it as two kids doing a homework assignment; we were there to get a job done, and that was our only thought. We were not intimate again for the rest of the month.

When Yanina returned to the gynecologist a month later, she was pregnant. We sat with her gynecologist as we might a priest: we were somewhat awed by his uncanny ability to bestow pregnancy. We both felt a curious blend of excitement and caution. Based on our past history, we were both fearful. Over the ensuing weeks, the doctor kept a very close eye on Yanina. Through a sonogram we had found out we were expecting a girl.

After 23 ½ weeks (around the same time Yanina had gone into labor with James), she went into labor again with our new daughter. Yanina was sent to Vassar Brothers Hospital in Poughkeepsie, where James had lived and died. Neither of us wanted to be back there again. But this time the doctors were able to stop the labor, and after a week Yanina was sent home to complete bed rest.

At 31 weeks, our daughter wanted out. We again found ourselves at Northern Dutchess Hospital in Rhinebeck, just like 17 months before with James. Since Yanina was again premature, the neonatal doctor and nurse were called in from Vassar Brothers in Poughkeepsie.

Before they could arrive, a C-section was performed and, on October 22, 2001, our daughter was born. There were complications: our baby was very purple, and the doctors had difficulty getting her to breathe. Everyone in the room knew we had lost a son not long before. When our little girl took her first breath I nearly fell to my knees. She was put in an incubator and we were told she would be taken to Vassar, just as James had been.

This was too much déjà vu for any of us, but it got worse. Later, while I was in the room with Yanina, the staff came in to show us our daughter. With them was the same doctor who Yanina had told only last year, "Thank you so much for taking care of our son, and no offense, but I hope I never see you again." But here we were, looking at the same doctor, with our daughter taking the same ride baby James had taken.

Again my wife was in one hospital, my baby in another, and my three boys at home. I left Yanina, went home to tell my boys about their sister, and off I went to Vassar Hospital. If there is one place in the world you don't want to be well-known, a regular customer, it is in the neonatal intensive care unit. All the nurses remembered me, I knew all the desk staff and doctors. When I went to see our girl, she was plugged in to as many tubes as James had been. It was a sight I almost couldn't bear. But the doctors told us her chances of survival were much better than 50-50, and she was a much bigger baby than James.

I did the same run-around I had done before. I spent time with my wife while she was still in the hospital, took care as best I could of my three boys at home, and spent as much time with baby Lauryn as possible. We were told that most babies stay in the neonatal unit until their actual due date, and so that meant Lauryn would be there for two months. When I visited on the sixth day I got scrubbed up, put on my gown and went into the room.

She was gone.

If I had looked down at the floor and saw my heart there, bloodied and beating, fallen right out my chest, I would not have been surprised. I could not believe that we could lose another child.

One of the nurses saw me and rushed in. "Mr. Bay, Lauryn was doing so much better she was moved to another unit."

I was able to feed my little girl some breast milk I had brought from my wife.

On Halloween, a few days later, we received a call from the hospital. Yanina, who in the meantime had come home for bed rest, answered the phone. "Mrs. Bay, come and get your daughter. She's eating us out of house and home."

Here I was again at a neonatal unit. The doors were locked, so I pushed the button.

"Can I help you?"

"I'm here to see Jenesis Campbell."

"One moment please."

The woman behind the counter buzzed me in. When I walked in, she said, "Every time I hear someone ask to see Jenesis, right away I think of the Bible."

"I'm her uncle, and I think of it sometimes too when I hear her name."

"You go down to the end of the hall, take a left, and then it will be the fifth door on your right."

Off I went to see the new baby. After I settled into a chair, Jenesis and Chris and I talked for a while about Elliot's birth. I took a few pictures with my cell phone. After a while Jenesis wanted to take a shower, so while she and Chris were in the bath, the lady who had buzzed me into the unit came into the room to make the bed. She stripped the bed and then started making it. I could tell she had made a great many beds in her day. And I was impressed at the result: all the creases were sharp, and if you dropped a coin on the sheets that coin would have bounced as if on a trampoline.

"You really make a mean bed," I told her. "How long have you been doing this job?"

"Thirty-something years and I've loved every minute of it."

"That's a long time to do a job."

"I was in the service before this job and that's where I learned my bed making skills."

"You must have been here when my kids were born."

"What's the last name?"

"Bay."

"I don't quite remember that name."

"I wasn't sure you would with all the babies that have been born in this hospital."

"So you're the uncle?"

"I'm Jenesis' uncle. The new baby's great-uncle. I don't know what makes me feel older, being a great-uncle or the injuries from my fall."

"What happened? Were you in a car accident?"

"Believe or not, I free-fell 14 feet off of a road into a culvert."

She looked at me, confused. "You fell off a road? How does someone fall off a road?"

I told her the short version, and, as I do with everyone, when I came to God I said, "I don't know if you believe in God or not, but I met Him at the road that night."

She smiled. "Oh I believe, there's no doubt about that."

She finished the bed and was getting ready to leave. I told her, "My friend Mickey and I have a book written about it."

"What's the title going to be?"

"Miracle on Hammertown Road."

She gathered up her things and at the door she said, "That's a good title, because it's a miracle you're here to share your story. Thank you for sharing it with me."

"That's what God wants me to do, even it's one person at a time. Now you didn't forget the title of the book did you?"

"I'm going to go write it down now."

Jenesis came out of the shower and I spent another twenty minutes with everyone and then decided it was time to say my goodbyes.

As I approached the nurse's station, I saw the nurse who had made Jenesis' bed speaking to three other nurses. "Ah," she said as I got near, "here he is, the man I was telling you all about."

At that point they all gathered around and asked questions.

"When do you think your book will come out?"

"I'm not sure about that, but I'll be trying to get it published."

Then one of the nurses said, "You *do* know you told your story to the right lady first, right?"

"Why is that?"

"Well, you know she's a nun."

I turned and looked with surprise at the woman who had been in the service, who had made Jenesis' bed with military precision, who had told me, 'Oh I believe, there's no doubt about that.'

"You didn't mention that little detail to me."

"Well, just like you probably don't tell everyone about meeting God, I don't tell everyone I'm a nun."

"You've got a point there."

We chatted a bit more before it was time for me to go. The nun told me, "Thank you again for telling me your story, you really *have* made my day."

"Thank you," I told her. "And you've made mine."

As I walked out of the hospital I knew why that voice in church had told me to go to the hospital. I not only got to see my niece and grand-niece, but also, for the first time, told my story to a small group of people. And I knew: there is more to everyone, and everything, than meets the eye.

Man, Do I Have a Story for You

Well we are in the homestretch and it definitely feels good to be almost out of school. Thanks for all the help you have given me through the years, not only in schoolwork but also in just being there when I needed you the most. I am so happy that you are my best friend.

So began the nearly eight pages that Bubba filled in my high school senior yearbook. I wrote as many pages in his. Before we signed each other's yearbooks, Bubba and I made a pact: we would write down everything we could remember that we had done together through Junior High and High school. And so those pages in my yearbook are filled with snapshots of our friendship- studying for the SATs and laughing ourselves silly about dangling participles, Bubba getting a basketball rebound while flat on his back, me dressed up as a Harlem Globetrotter for Halloween.

Maybe we looked an odd couple- I was tall and skinny, and Bubba was, well, exactly what a guy nicknamed Bubba should look like- but we were best friends. We studied together, played sports together, went out to eat together, hung out together in and out of school. Bubba's house was in town not far from the high school, so before basketball games I would go over and his mom would cook for us. Bubba's home became a second home for me, and mine for him.

Our yearbook predicted, tongue-in-cheek, that '10 Years From Now' I would be 'a Canadian guide married to a squaw.' Bubba, the prognosticators said, would be a 'business manager at Jamesbay'. But needless to say, I never married a squaw and Bubba never became a business manager. Do any of us, at age 18, have even an inkling of where our lives will lead us? On page 234, scribbled across a picture of our classmate Fuzzy McClinton, Bubba wrote: All I can say is that through the rest of our lives we had better keep in touch. *But sadly, despite all our youthful enthusiasm, we didn't keep in touch. Like so many high school friends, Bubba and I grew apart over the years. My own road didn't lead me to Canada, but to Thailand, where now, 30 years after high school graduation, I live in Bangkok, where I am a lecturer at a university. I wasn't around for most of the events in Bubba's adult life- the death of his baby son James, the death of his stepson Robert, his eventual divorce from Yanina, his move to Arizona and move back to New York. I was in town for his son Logan's first birthday party, and though I don't have a strong memory of it, I was invited but did not attend. It wasn't until many years later that Bubba told me how upset he was that I hadn't gone to his little boy's birthday. I don't remember why I didn't go. Maybe I was working at the time; maybe I had something else to do that night; maybe I simply didn't feel like going. To be perfectly honest, I don't remember being invited at all. It's a painful reminder to me of how we get wrapped up in our own lives. After that, Bubba and I didn't have much contact for the next 10 years. I wasn't often in New York, and we didn't write or e-mail. To me it seemed like we had simply drifted apart as high school friends so often do, but I think to Bubba it felt a little worse than that.*

135

Not long after November 15, 2009, I logged onto the computer in my university office and read an e-mail sent by Denise (Bartholf) Loveland and Julie Gillis, who have done the workhorse's share of keeping the Stissing Mountain High School Class of '83 in touch with each other. The e-mail said that Bubba had fallen and had broken a great number of bones and was fighting for his life. Though I was half a world away, gazing out the window at palm trees and rice paddies, a thousand images of my life with Bubba flashed through my mind. It was a life that, quite suddenly, did not feel so very far away. I logged onto the Caring Bridge website and wrote a few comments of support. I started e-mailing Bub when I knew he was out of rehab and home, telling him I might be in New York some time in 2010, maybe in April, maybe in August, maybe for Christmas. It was often like this for me. My trips to New York depended on my schedule at university, and the cost of a plane ticket from Bangkok to New York was often through the roof. But I did make it home, in September.

A day or two after I arrived in New York I went up to the Stanford Cemetery, where so many of my family are buried. My Uncle John Alterio had recently passed away, and I was looking for his headstone. My mom had given me some idea where it was, but as I wandered through those headstones- stopping to pay my respects to my grandmother Liz, my grandfather Chub, my great grandmother Rose, my great Uncle Eddie, some kids who had died young in high school- I couldn't find my Uncle John. On the far side of the cemetery I saw two men digging a grave. One of them I recognized as John Bay, and the other was Bubba. I had only been home a day or two and was still jetlagged, and hadn't called Bub yet. I walked over, said hi, and Bubba told me their landscaping business was contracted to dig graves here, along with mowing. I looked at the tiny grave they were digging. A child's grave. I could only imagine how it must affect Bubba to dig graves for children, but I didn't say anything. I told him I was having trouble finding my Uncle John's grave. He said his brother John had dug that one, and after John told us where to look, Bubba and I walked and caught up quickly on our news. I told him I had recently finished writing a novel and was hoping to get it published. "A novel? So you're a writer now?" It was then that Bubba told me, "Man, do I have a story for you."

We met later that week and went for a walk near the Hudson River at the Poet's Walk, Bubba walking slowly and carefully with his cane, and he told me about the night of his fall. I expected to hear about the broken bones and rehab, the things I'd read about on the Caring Bridge website and had heard from my parents and friends. But Bubba had much more to tell me that day. "Yeah," I told him, "do you ever have a story to tell." It didn't take me long to think it over, and I told him I'd try my best to help him write his book.

Over the ensuing weeks we met over pizza, or at his house, or at my parent's, or for walks or movies. It was almost like old times. After so many years, I was coming to know my best friend from high school better than I ever thought I would again. Bubba would talk and I would take notes, or he would write as best he could and e-mail me. Sometimes he would give me scraps of paper covered with his chicken-scratch handwriting. I'm probably one of the few people in the world who can decipher Bubba's handwriting; even in high school I could do it. In my yearbook, page 239, Bubba wrote:

I'll cherish the memories, and someday I'll tell my kids all the crazy things we did. The only way we could be closer is if we were brothers. There's so much more to say, but I'd have to write a book.

Now Bubba has his book, but more importantly he has his life, and his friends and family. And he has God.

While we were writing, Bubba would often point to his head and tell me he had trouble thinking straight after his fall, to forgive him if he stuttered his words or had trouble getting things out. But there was nothing to forgive, either from him or from me. Despite slowly drifting apart over 25 years, we had come upon each other again in a cemetery, surrounded by the souls of those who had departed. It is a miracle that Bubba had not joined them that night in November 2009. Here he was, alive and telling his story, and here I was having flown 12,000 miles. Somehow, we had found each other again.

- Mickey Ruzich

137

Caring Bridge website- Guestbook:

Sunday, January 3, 2010

Bubba,

So glad you are home!!! Physical Therapy is tough, but you can do it! Stay strong and positive and keep the faith. You are a miracle of God. We will continue to pray for your full recovery.

Connie H.

Monday, January 4, 2010

Happy New Year Jimmy!

We are so happy to hear that you are home. Thought of you often through the holidays and praying for you to remain strong. Though the road ahead may be a tough one, we know you are up to the challenge, you have been a miracle from day one! Our thoughts and prayers are with you and your family always.

Ken & Nancy H.

My friends did not say 'it' was a miracle; they did not even say that climbing up out of that ditch was a miracle. They said *I* was a miracle.

Me.

Bubba.

Every life has its mistakes, its regrets, its terrible tragedies. God knows I've had my share. I've been down in the pit, almost as deep as a person can go. There were times when I couldn't see any light at all from where I was. But I climbed up out of there, time and time again. Some friends tell me it's a miracle, after all that has happened to me- after the deaths of my boys, two divorces, my lifelong struggle with my weight, financial problems, a fall that should by rights have killed me- that I still give praise to God. People often ask me if there have been times in my life, with my face upturned to the heavens, when I have cried out to God, "Why me?" My answer is that, odd as it may seem to some, I have almost never asked that question. Partly because no matter how bad you think you have it, there are always many who have it much worse. Since my accident I have met so many people who are also meeting terrible challenges. After they talk to me they often say, "I don't have it as bad as

I thought"; I can only shake my head in wonder because I'm usually thinking the same thing. And I believe that God gives no one more than anyone can handle. But more than anything, over the past years, through all the tragedies and struggles in my life, I have learned something surprising: everything is a miracle. Albert Einstein said there are two ways to live your life: one is as though nothing is a miracle; the other is as though everything is a miracle. After my accident, I see that everything is a miracle. No matter your religion, no matter what God you believe in, or whether you believe in God at all. Simply breathing, seeing, tasting, touching, are miracles. Taking a hot shower is a miracle. The brightening sky in the early morning is a miracle. Being in good health is a miracle.

I feel blessed. I was blessed to be with my baby son James Ulysses for the ten days he was on earth, blessed to become Robert's dad and spend the time with him I did. I even feel blessed to have had the financial problems I've had, because I've learned that things may be good one day, but all it takes is one event to turn your world upside down. And I even feel blessed to have fallen on Hammertown Road and shattered my body because that night God came to me in my need. November 15 is an anniversary for me now, but no longer only one of painful memories; if anything, it feels more like a second birthday.

I have been given a new pair of eyes. I have learned to see people differently. I can recognize in others' eyes a deep need to talk, to share, a need to simply be with someone. And so these new eyes have also given me new ears. I listen. You can never know what someone has been through until you listen. I open my heart and listen to what others have to say, and often the conversation comes around to what happened to me. We are all put on this earth with one pair of feet, so we can only walk our own path. Some roads I might have taken in my life are now blocked, closed off for good. But at the same time I am blessed to be walking at all, down new roads, with new eyes and ears, with a new lease on life and with God walking alongside me.

Before my accident, I would feel badly whenever I heard about someone who was paralyzed or had a neck, back or brain injury. But now when I hear those things it strikes very close to the bone. It is, in fact, a miracle that I walked to my neighbor's house that night despite 23 broken bones. It is, in fact, a miracle I am still walking at all after having 13 fractures on my spine and neck. In rehab and since I have heard many stories of people who were up on a step- ladder changing a light bulb, who fell and fractured one or two vertebrae and ended up paralyzed for life. I don't understand why I am able to walk while so many others, with less severe injuries than mine, cannot. I get up every morning, sore and stiff and groaning like a man much older than 48, but simply putting my feet on the floor is a blessing, a miracle. I thank God for it. When I was in the hospital, I told myself that I will never again be the man I used to be, that I would probably never again be 100%. But whatever percentage God wants me to be, I'll take it.

In the Bible, we are told of some amazing miracles: parting the Red Sea, walking on water, turning water into wine, feeding 5,000 with seven loaves, water from a stone, the healing of lepers and the blind, the dead coming back to life. But most of us will never see burning bushes, we will never see the sun stopped in the sky. We will not have a conversation with God or be instructed to bring tablets down from the Mount. We will wake up tomorrow and struggle to pay our bills and put a good meal on the table for our children. That is the life God has given us. And I see now, that is enough. Simple acts- buying a jacket for my son, being able to get around the house without a walker- are as heroic, as miraculous, as anything anyone in the world will ever do. I only regret that it took such a drastic event to help me see that every single thing is so full of God that it is about to burst.

It is a miracle that God came to me in my hour of need. It is a miracle that God spoke to me, told me I would live and that my life had purpose. Like the doctors who were on call for me when I was in the hospital, I am on call now for God. When God needs me, He will call me and I will answer and do the work He wants me to do. And so my meeting with God on Hammertown Road that night did not end when God walked away in the Light. The meeting continues. Throughout the day, deep into the night, I listen for God.

When my family moved to Pine Plains we attended the Methodist Church, though I had been baptized Episcopalian. My folks bought a fixer-upper of a house, and Sunday was my Dad's only day off, so instead of singing hymns or sitting in pews, on Sundays we swung a lot of hammers. Throughout most of my life I attended church only sporadically. But now I go almost every Sunday, and have even become a trustee. I still don't know the Bible well, but when my Pastor gives a sermon, I often feel like shouting out- *I can testify to that!* With my own eyes I have seen the truth of many of the words my Pastor speaks. I don't go to church to be with God, because I know for certain that God is everywhere, even on Hammertown Road overlooking a 14-foot drop into a concrete culvert.

I'm not special. I'm not rich, not famous, I don't have any special talents. I'm not even a good practicing Christian. But God came to me all the same. It is sometimes overwhelming to realize I saw God, to have had the experience I had. Why me? Maybe because I am just Bubba Bay, and if God is there for Bubba Bay, then God is there for you, too. Maybe that's what God wants us all to know.

On November 15, 2009, I spent most of the day at an old farmhouse my friend Jack owned doing my favorite hobby, metal-detecting. I don't remember what I found, if anything, that day at Jack's place. But after I was done metal-detecting for the day, I went home, had a tuna special, felt a bit sick, and went for a walk on Hammertown Road. I fell into a ravine, cracked open my skull and broke my body. And then I saw the most beautiful thing I have ever seen.

One thing I've learned from metal-detecting: you might find the most beautiful treasure buried in the most surprising places. Buried deep under old foundations, or in lawns or in fields, on beaches or alongside old wood roads, I have found the most wonderful coins and buttons and bottles and rings. And buried deep within my own pain and hurt, inside my sadness at the loss of my sons, within my own broken bones and shattered spirit, I have found God.

Author's Notes

(1) Visit *www.jimbubbabay.com* for more information about this book and Bubba Bay, photos, links to other sites, and a place to share your own stories.

(2) A portion of the proceeds from all sales of this book will be donated to the Brain Injury Association of New York State, and to the Cognitive Skills Program for Brain Injury at the Putnam County ARC.

(3) For those readers interested in visiting the Caring Bridge website:

    (i)   Go to *www.caringbridge.com.*

    (ii)   Under 'Visit a Website', type jamesbay1

    (iii)   Enter your e-mail address

    (iv)   Create a password of your choosing, enter your name and accept the Terms of Agreement

    (v)   You may now navigate around the site. There are Journal entries, Guestbook comments, and pictures.

Please consider supporting the Caring Bridge organization.

(4) Please consider supporting the Make-A-Wish Foundation, an organization that gives so many families with terminally ill children, including mine, experiences to remember forever.

Acknowledgements

My sincerest thanks:

To the Caring Bridge organization, for offering a free service to people in need, and whose webpage on my behalf brought me more comfort than I can express.

To the many people who wrote comments of support to me on my Caring Bridge website. Your words mean more to me than you know.

To all the many medical and other professionals who helped save my life.

To my mom and dad, for their love and support and for always being there.

To my brother, John, one of my best friends in this world.

To my sister-in-law Mary Ann, for all she did and continues to do.

To my sister, Diana, who gave me pedicures, washed my hair, helped me shave, drove me to appointments and food shopping, and who rekindled our relationship after some tough times.

To my ex-wife Yanina, for her love and support over many years, and for sharing her story.

To my children, Jon and Logan and Lauryn, and Robert and James Ulysses. You are my world.

To my Aunt Barbara, for all her research into rehab units and for coming to see me when I needed to see a friendly face.

To my cousin TJ, for driving up 3 hours from New Jersey, and for bringing two of the biggest bags of fast food from McDonald's I have ever seen. My stomach is still hurting.

To my friend Jack McDonald, for his acts of kindness. I will never forget his help.

To my friend Rick Stuetzle, for friendship since elementary school and dinners every time he is in town.

To my Aunt Lois, for her generous spirit and help over the years.

To my cousin Veronica Brenner Walsh, who has also lost a child, for her support and for sharing her story.

To my cousins Michael and Kevin, for all their help and support.

To Linda and Joe for their visits, their warm blanket and warm hat.

To my friend Lonnie, whose visits over the many weeks I was laid up meant the world to me.

To Eric Duffy, for his friendship and encouraging me to write about my story.

To Kevin Feeney, who visited me often and fixed my car.

To Mom and Pops Ruzich, who brought nuts that I enjoyed in rehab, but that my many guests enjoyed even more.

To Dr. Bruce Wilkinson, author of 'The Prayer of Jabez'. To this day, I have no idea how that book ended up in my packing box.

To Dr. Lois Tannenbaum, Board President, Brain Injury Association of New York State and Director of Brain Injury Services, Putnam ARC, for helping me cope with my brain injury, and for her contribution to this book.

To my friend Mickey Ruzich (just like I will always be Bubba to him, he will always be Mickey to me), for his friendship. Without him this book would not have been written.

To Pastor Greg Higgins of the United Methodist Church in Pine Plains, New York, for inspiring sermons and spiritual guidance.

To Indira Velasquez, Rich Brenner, Jenesis Campbell, Geoffrey Talcott, Donna Philipbar, Dominic Vigna, and Domenica Biro, for contributing to this book. This book is all the better, as is my life, for their presence in it.

To all those I have not named but who visited me and sent me their wishes and prayers.

Last but certainly not least, I would like to thank God.

Appendix

In a Moment...The Occurrence and Persistence of Brain Injury

By Lois Tannenbaum, PsyD, CBIS, LEND Fellow, M.Ed
Board President of the Brain Injury Association of New York State
Director of Brain Injury Program @ Putnam ARC

As a brain injury survivor, caregiver, and professional in the field, I am impressed and touched by the story *Miracle on Hammertown Road* written by Jim Bubba Bay. It provides a true accounting as to how he fell 12 feet head first into a ravine and landed on rocks, hitting the left side of his head first, then left shoulder and rib area. Total injuries: fractured skull, brain bleed, TBI (traumatic brain injury), concussion, fractured neck, fractured back, fractured shoulder, fractured ribs. Overall, there were 23 bones involved with 26 fractures. This gripping, true story truly hits home the point that brain injury can strike anyone, anywhere, anytime quite suddenly and unexpectedly in a moment that changes a person's lifetime.

Brain injury is not new, it is just better understood and identified. Scrolls written as early as 1650-1550 BC describe various head injuries and symptoms. The term concussion began to be more widely used in the 16th century. Over the years, there have been technological advances in imaging diagnostic tools that assist in early identification and intervention. Public awareness increased in the 1970s, and the 1990s were deemed the "Decade of the Brain." The more science advances, the more we learn about the causes of deficits and personality changes related to brain injury.

Have we come full circle? Not by a long shot! Despite awareness campaigns and protective equipment, there are so many causal factors related to brain injury. It is not a particular event, or an illness that can be cured. The only cure is prevention. Moreover, brain injury can be classified as one of the cradle to grave disabilities, and can occur at anytime across the lifespan, striking as an injury or an illness. Brain injury can range from mild to severe, and its effects can be temporary or permanent, transforming it from an occurrence to a lifelong disability.

In fact, the incidence and prevalence of brain injury is such that it has been deemed the "silent epidemic." Over the last few years, the incidence of brain injury has increased from 1 every 23 seconds to 1 every 13 seconds: babies who fall, or whose heads are badly shaken; young children and teens involved in sports or other activities; seniors with balance issues that result in falls; and every age in between if faced with an accident or health issues. Brain injury does not discriminate! It is an equal opportunity disability among all ages, genders, and ethnic groups.

Brain injury impacts 5.3 million people each year. In New York alone, the lives of 400 individuals per day are affected along with the lives of their families. As stated by the Brain Injury Association of America, "Brain injury is not an event or an outcome. It is the start of a misdiagnosed, misunderstood, under-funded neurological disease. Individuals who sustain brain injuries must have timely access to expert trauma care, specialized rehabilitation, lifelong disease management and individualized services and supports in order to live healthy, independent and satisfying lives." The financial toll of brain injury amounts to over $76 billion annually while the toll on the lives of people impacted by this disability is immeasurable.

Brain injury has received increased attention related to issues in the national sport of football from Pee Wee Leagues to the National Football League. In addition, in light of the high numbers of military personnel sustaining traumatic brain injuries related to IED Blast Wounds, brain injury has been deemed the signature wound of the wars in Iraq and Afghanistan, affecting over 400,000 service members. A residual effect for many has been post-concussion syndrome, or post trauma syndrome, resulting in more young military service members dying by suicide than on the battlefield, now calculated at 22 lost lives per day.

It has been said, "If you've seen one brain injury, then you've seen one brain injury." This is so true because no two people are affected in the exact same way. The effects may be physical, cognitive, or behavioral/emotional and may include:

Physical Effects	Cognitive Effects	Behavioral Effects
Loss of Smell and Taste	Short Term/Working Memory	Impulsivity
Hearing Loss	Attention	Emotional Lability
Visual Difficulties	Concentration	Irritability
Balance Difficulties	Distractibility	Decreased Frustration Tolerance
Dysarthria	Decreased Verbal Fluency/Comprehension	Impaired Judgment
Motor Control and Coordination	Information processing	Tension/Anxiety
Fatigue	Arousal	Depression
Seizures	Problem Solving	Aggressive Behaviors
Decreased Tolerance/Drugs and Alcohol	Changed Intellectual Functioning	Disinhibition
Headaches	Abstraction and Conceptualization	Changed Sexual Drive
Sleep Disturbances	Slowed Reaction Time	Changed Personality

The most common symptoms usually described by individuals who have sustained a brain injury are difficulty planning and organizing. This is related to damage to the brain impacting executive functioning skills such as goal setting, self-monitoring, planning, initiating, modifying, and completing.

The various deficit areas listed above greatly affect people's lives as well as their interactions with others. Their relationship with themselves may become very defeated or negative. Their self-esteem and self-confidence may become unsure due to real or perceived loss of ability which in turn affects motivation. A sense of profound loss for the person they may have been can become a huge barrier to moving forward. In addition to grieving the loss of former self, people can become very angry for what they believe they can no longer do or accomplish. These feelings do not happen in isolation. Anger and depression touch many lives at home, in the workplace, and in the community.

In life after brain injury, normalcy does not resume, it is reconstructed. People learn strategies to compensate for the areas and functions that have been affected. They begin to focus on their strengths and interests, accessing programs, services, and support groups. With the help of organizations like the Brain Injury Association of NYS (BIANYS) and the Putnam ARC (PARC) brain injury program, slowly, but steadily life transforms into a "new normal."